LUCIFER
DID ME
A FAVOR

VOLUME VI

Pastor Don R. Vining

Leavitt Peak Press

ISBN: 978-1-969865-70-1 (sc)
ISBN: 978-1-969865-71-8 (e)

Rev. date: 12/06/2025

FOREWORD

Lucifer was Heaven's chief worshipper—beautiful, gifted, and radiant with the glory of God. But pride entered his heart, and he thought he could take over God's throne. Jesus said in **Luke 10:18**, *"I saw Satan fall like lightning from Heaven."* Lucifer, along with one-third of Heaven's angels, fell from grace.

Be careful who you follow, because even the most glorious can fall.

After Lucifer's rebellion, God created man and placed him in the Garden of Eden. Yet man, too, fell from grace. But God, in His mercy, sent Jesus—the second Adam—who took on the form of man. He lived among us, suffered like us, and died as one of us. But on the third day, He rose again, unlike any mortal man.

To silence all doubt, He appeared to His disciples. He ate with them. They saw His wounds and touched His hands. He did not rise as a ghost or a spirit, but in glorified flesh. Then, He ascended into Heaven with a promise that He would return again.

Because He bore the cross and conquered death, we have been set free from the sin that once separated us from God. And when He returns, there will be *a new Heaven and a new Earth*. We will be reunited with all those we love, forever in His presence.

Lucifer did us a favor, because while he lost the privilege of worship, **we gained it**. We can now worship the Almighty God in spirit and in truth. What Lucifer forfeited, we inherited.

DEDICATION

This book is lovingly dedicated to our awesome grandchildren— **Aubrey**, 17, a talented catcher and soon-to-be high school graduate;

London, 14, a fiery and gifted pitcher with an unstoppable spirit;

Blaze, 14 going on 25, a young entrepreneur and a true chip off the old block;

Greyson, 9, learning to play the guitar and always ready for the ball field, who loves to sit on the porch and ask me questions; and

Declan, 6, bright and full of curiosity, who loves math and spelling, and just might become President someday.

My greatest desire for each of you is this: that you build a strong, personal relationship with **Jesus Christ**, and come to know the **magnificent Heaven** that awaits those who love Him. One day, we will all be together there for eternity- rejoicing, worshipping, and celebrating the One who made it possible.

INTRODUCION

God's A to Z Plan — Understanding the Flow of Worship

As I continue my life-long journey of learning about this God I serve, and as I have dealt with people on a daily basis as a Pastor, I find there is a lack of understanding about how worship comes from Heaven to earth and moves back to Heaven. I call it **God's A to Z Plan.**

This plan has nothing to do with what organization or denomination you may or may not be a part of—whether you are Baptist, Catholic, Presbyterian, Pentecostal, etc.—or whether you are a long-term believer or are new to the Faith. It's about having a **Christian heart**.

Most of us know there is a God and that God is a Spirit and that we should worship Him.

John 4:24 says: *"God is a Spirit: and they that worship him must worship him in spirit and in truth."*

But we're often not sure what that means or how it works in our everyday lives.

From Heaven's Worship to Earth's Creation

As we move through this book together, we will find that God had total worship in Heaven until Lucifer decided he wanted to take over the throne of God. Therefore, Lucifer and one-third of the stars (angels) were kicked out of Heaven and fell to the earth.

At that point, God began another chapter of His plan. He created man and placed him in the Garden of Eden—an earthly paradise surrounded by four rivers that would give man everything he needed for life and fulfillment. God even gave the first man, Adam, a help-mate—Eve—so that His creation could experience relationship, unity, and purpose.

The Fall and the Promise of Redemption

As we will find, Adam fell because he did not obey God. Therefore, God had to send the second Adam, who was Jesus Christ. Jesus lived His life on earth to show man what God the Creator was all about, His love, His compassion, His truth, and His desire to restore what was lost.

Christ then gave His life on the Cross so that man would have the hope of eternal salvation.

I like to say it this way, **from the cradle, to the cross, to the crown.**

Meaning that those who accept Jesus Christ as Lord and Savior will spend eternity in a place called **Heaven**, also known as the **New Jerusalem**.

An Invitation to Discover God's Incredible Plan

I invite you to come with me on this journey that will show you just how incredible God's plan is for our lives. Together, we will see how even Lucifer's rebellion became part of a divine orchestration that revealed God's wisdom, power, and unchanging love.

Through every rise and fall, through every act of creation and redemption, we'll discover that **God's A to Z Plan** was never interrupted, it was only revealed in stages so that you and I could learn what true worship, grace, and calling are all about.

CHAPTER 1

WHAT GOD NEEDS

The True Focus of Worship

Christians throughout the world believe and understand that our God likes to be worshipped, but I am not sure we understand the importance of worship, or its significance.

Quite frankly, I always thought the most valuable thing that could happen in ministry was to find a sinner (that is, a person who is lost and dying and going to a devil's hell), snatch him out of the pit of hell, and introduce him to the saving grace of Jesus Christ.

While that is so very important, I'm not sure it should be our main focus.

It's not that evangelism loses value, it's that worship becomes the foundation from which everything else flows.

Does that shock you? Let me explain.

When True Worship Takes Place

When worship, true worship, takes place, the Lord, by His Spirit, will send the message of salvation to those who are lost, hurting, and dying in sin.

I believe if we engage in heartfelt, continuous worship, the sinner is going to be reached. The focus has always been on reaching the unsaved, and that's vitally important.

But if we change our focus, if we go after God first—He is going to come after us.

If we go after God, He's going to come and heal our bodies. Actually, He's already healed our bodies; we're just not convinced that we've been healed.

Luke 19:10 says, *"For the Son of man is come to seek and to save that which was lost."*

When we worship the true God who is true to His word, and in that sense take care of His business, He will take care of our business.

Instead of bombarding the heavens with something we need, we're going to bombard the heavens with something **God needs.**

What God Needs

Did you know God has a need, a desire, an urgent longing?

We've always been taught that God has everything because He is everything. That's true, and yet He doesn't have worship unless we give Him worship.

Our God needs, desires, and expects worship from us.

John 4:23 tells us, *"But the hour cometh, and now is, when the true worshippers shall worship the Father in spirit and in truth: for the Father seeketh such to worship him."*

That's the reason He created us.

The Creator of the universe placed in us the one thing He Himself cannot manufacture — a freely offered heart of worship.

The need and desire can't be met unless we meet it.

In Luke 19:40, Jesus said, *"I tell you that, if these should hold their peace, the stones would immediately cry out."*

He meant that the rocks would cry out in praise if we don't.

God Hears Worshippers

John 9:31 makes an interesting statement: *"Now we know that God heareth not sinners: but if any man be a worshipper of God, and doeth his will, him he heareth."*

The word *"sinners"* here means those who have an attitude against anything that is of God.

If you have the wrong attitude about worship, that is a sin, and God does not hear sinners.

John continues, *"But if any man be a worshipper of God and doeth His will, him He heareth."*

He hears us, if we do His will. That's the criteria.

Worship aligns the heart with heaven so that prayer becomes communication, not complaint.

Growing Beyond Immaturity in Faith

We should be long past the "crybaby" and "poor little old me" stage.

It's time to quit wondering why God blessed someone across the street and not us.

It's time to get serious about our relationship with God. We don't have six months to find Him; we need to be about His business now.

There are a lot of ministries that have been experiencing God, but they don't understand that it is God. They think it is good music or great preaching. It isn't.

It is the Spirit of the Lord responding to those who worship Him.

God Doesn't Hear Sinners, But He Hears Worshippers

God doesn't hear sinners, but if you worship God, He hears you. He hears those who worship Him.

Let me clarify this for you. God hears the voice of the sinner who cries out, "God, have mercy upon my soul."

The thief on the cross next to Christ said, *"Have mercy on me."*

What did Jesus say? *"Today shalt thou be with me in Paradise."* (Luke 23:43)

Someone came to me recently and asked, "Pastor, do we have to speak in tongues to make it to heaven?"

Did the thief on the cross speak in tongues? I think not. Did he say, "I'll dress better, look better, give more money, or do this or that?"

No. He said, "Master, have mercy on me."

And mercy, at that moment, he received.

That's the salvation message: *Lord, have mercy on my dear lost soul.*

He says, *"My child, mercy, it shall be."*

King Saul's Worship

The Old Testament only records one instance where King Saul worshipped God.

1 Samuel 15:31: *"So Samuel turned again after Saul; and Saul worshipped the LORD."*

The Bible says that he actually worshipped God all night long.

Would it interrupt our plans if we had to worship God all night long?

That night, when the musicians and singers began to sing psalms of praise to God, it became a big spiritual thing in King Saul's life. He had what we call a hoedown—and God showed up.

But it was a one-time thing. You don't read anywhere else about King Saul worshipping God in that manner.

He thought he could live forty years with just one incident, one encounter, one major contact with God.

That's where a lot of Christians live. They think, *"Well, I experienced God today, so that will last me for the next 52 weeks."*

But God is not a one-encounter kind of God; He desires ongoing relationship through worship.

God's Constant Presence

God wants us to experience Him every time we come together.

He is not a part-time God. He isn't a God who says, "I'll show up when you need Me."

He said, *"I will never leave thee nor forsake thee."* (Hebrews 13:5)

He said that no matter where you are, what you are going through, or what church you attend, He's there.

He's in it for the duration. Take it to the bank; draw interest on it— He's there for you.

> *Worship doesn't summon God; it awakens our awareness that He's already present.*

God Will Not Let Anything Stay Close to Him That Does Not Worship

God will not let anything stay close to Him that does not repetitively worship Him.

Do you have the desire to be close to God? I mean, really have that desire?

Then get busy worshipping Him every day.

He is not going to allow you to get close to Him if you do not worship Him on an ongoing basis. It has to become a habit.

Becoming Habitual Worshippers

I know of a young man who went before a judge for a speeding citation. The judge said,

> *"Young man, if you come before me again for this reason, I'm going to list you as a habitual offender."*

"So, what does that mean?" the young man asked.

"That means you are going to lose your license for five years."

That young man decided he wasn't going to be a habitual offender, so he slowed down.

God would love for us to be **habitual worshippers**.

He wants our worship every time we come together. We say, *"Lord, we're desperate for You."*

God is desperate for our worship.

Worship is not a *charismatic thing*. Worship is a *Bible thing*.

When we worship, we are doing what the Bible says.

You've heard the old saying, *"Time is of the essence."* I want to tell you that **worship is of the essence.**

We need God, we need God now—and the only way we get God now is to worship Him now.

The most important thing we can do is not to give money, sing songs, or preach a word.

The most important thing we can do is to come in and worship.

Worship is critical.

Faith That Moves Mountains

In Matthew 21:21 we read:

> *"Jesus answered and said unto them, Verily I say unto you, If ye have faith, and doubt not, ye shall not only do this which is done to the fig tree, but also if ye shall say unto this mountain, Be thou removed, and be thou cast into the sea; it shall be done."*

Not long ago, I had an opportunity to travel in the mountains for a few days. I was ready to move there.

But what really amazed me was to think that I could look at a mountain and say, *"Mountain, get out of my way,"* and God could move it. He is that powerful.

Sometimes, though, God chooses not to move mountains.

Just like when road builders dig through solid rock, God will make a **tunnel through the mountain** if that is what it takes.

You are going to go from this side of darkness to that side of light.

Worship is what God uses to tunnel through our problems.

Worship Breaks Barriers

Do you have problems? Need answers? Need God to touch you physically?

God can use your worship to tunnel through what you need physically.

Worship is the most important—the most powerful—thing you can do.

The Story of Zacchaeus — And the Critics

I want you to notice something.

In Luke 19:10, we read the story of Jesus going to Zacchaeus' home.

The Bible says that when Jesus told Zacchaeus that He was going to his home, the people murmured.

People began to criticize Jesus because He was eating with publicans and sinners.

At times, people are going to criticize you for what you are doing for Christ.

Never mind them. Hold on. Keep doing what you've been doing and let God deal with the rest.

Focus on Worship, Not Opinions

Some time ago, someone said to me,

> *"Pastor, this person has a problem with how we do this, so maybe we need to cater to this and change how we do things."*

No, no, no, no, no.

It is time we focus on the single most important thing we can do, which is to worship, honor, magnify, and glorify Christ's name.

If we do that, His glory will show up and work in the lives of individuals.

People criticized Jesus. They murmured and complained—and it is still happening today.

We need to stay focused.

What Was Lost — and Why Jesus Came

Notice what Jesus said in Luke 19:10:

> *"For the Son of Man is come to seek and save that which was lost."*

He didn't say *"them"* or *"they"*—He said *"that."*

I believe something was lost in Heaven, and Jesus came not only to save sinners, but also to recover what was lost.

Jesus is not only after lost souls; He's after **worship**.

Recovering What Was Lost

Jesus came to save me from a life of death and from a devil's hell.

He came to seek and to save that which was lost.

When you lose something, you go find it and claim it back.

If someone humiliates your family, do you lie down like a dead gopher, or do you get up and go after them?

You say, *"Now, wait a minute. You've taken one step too far. This is my family, and you better get back on your side of the street."*

You take it back.

I believe Jesus came not only to seek the lost; He came to seek **that which was lost.**

What was lost? **Worship was lost.**

Salvation and Worship — Both Matter

Most of us were taught from birth that Jesus came just to save me.

I believed that salvation was the only reason He came.

Over and over we've heard, *"Praise God. Just walk the aisle, pray the prayer of repentance and Jesus will come into your heart. Be a good boy and a good girl, and Jesus is going to come back for you someday."*

That's all true, but I believe it's more than just getting saved.

It's more than just giving your heart to the Lord and renouncing sin in your life.

Renouncing sin is one of the privileges of Jesus giving His life on the cross, that's the reason He gave His life.

But I believe He also came to recover something that was stolen from Heaven.

Multiple Purposes of God's Touch

Jesus always has multiple reasons for touching your life.

Let's say you have a bad financial situation.

While you are concerned about the Lord touching your finances, there are multiple conversations going on in Heaven concerning you.

God is not setting us up by what He wants to do in our lives, He's already worked that work.

He's setting us up so that what we receive from Him today will prepare us for what He's going to be about tomorrow.

Worship today is often the preparation for revelation tomorrow.

Trusting God One Day at a Time

Some of us can't grasp that because we're so bound up in our minds.

We pray, *"Oh, if I can just get God to touch me right now."*

He's already touched you right now, my friend. You need to allow the manifestation of that truth.

Actually, I'm not concerned with right now, I'm already living in the "now."

I'm more concerned about whether I'll be granted another day on this earth.

"God, it's Your glory, mercy, and grace that I need for tomorrow. Lord, I need wisdom, not how to live the moment because I am already living the moment, but wisdom and the manifestation of the glory—which only comes by worship—to prepare me for what I'm about to step into."

Matthew 6:34 says,

> *"Take therefore no thought for the morrow: for the morrow shall take thought for the things of itself. Sufficient unto the day is the evil thereof."*

I'm not really interested in how we are going to handle today, we're already handling that.

I'm more concerned about tomorrow or next week or the month or year after that.

I want to make sure we're prepared. I want to make sure we received the message from yesterday to prepare us for tomorrow.

God Is Already at Work

God has multiple reasons, multiple ideas, and multiple conversations going on in Heaven on your behalf.

Are you trying to figure out what you are supposed to do for the next six months?

God is already working it out, friend.

Worship Him, and one day at a time, He will reveal the truth He has for you.

People say they're not going to move one bit until God shows them the plan.

Well then, you may sit there and rot.

If you knew what God was doing right now, you'd just goof it all up.

He shows us one day at a time.

An old song says, *"One day at a time, Sweet Jesus."*

There is a reason and an anointing in those words.

Living in the Now, Trusting for Tomorrow

I could care less what my life is going to look like six months, a year, or three or four years from now.

But I do have the understanding that God has granted me the grace, mercy, wisdom, and know-how to handle my life right now.

Thank God, He's talking in the heavens about what's going to happen next week or six months from now.

As soon as I get it in my head that God is in control, He will reveal what His will is for me.

He can't reveal His truth to me until I learn how to worship Him.

Worship is where the Lord speaks to us.

Heaven's Loss

Let's talk a bit about what was lost from Heaven that the Son of Man came to seek out on planet earth.

Take a moment first to read *Ezekiel 28* and *Isaiah 14* for some background.

The Bible says that Lucifer was Heaven's worship leader. In the Hebrew language, the word *"Lucifer"* means "light-bearer."

When he stood before the throne of God and worshipped God, Lucifer was not the light, but he was a bearer of light.

Understand, we are not the light, we never will be the light, but we are **bearers of the Light.**

Lucifer: The Light Bearer

Ezekiel 28:13 describes twelve beautiful stones that were part of Lucifer:

> *"Thou hast been in Eden the garden of God; every precious stone was thy covering, the sardius, topaz, and the diamond, the beryl, the onyx, and the jasper, the sapphire, the emerald, and the carbuncle, and gold: the workmanship of thy tabrets and of thy pipes was prepared in thee in the day that thou wast created."*

Imagine this with me. Lucifer was in Heaven, standing before the awesome God, worshipping Him.

All of a sudden, God expressed His light and the light hit Lucifer. Those twelve different stones would light up and shoot out of Lucifer like a Technicolor kaleidoscope.

In other words, there was some ricocheting going on.

You've heard of a .22 bullet hitting one wall but ricocheting and coming back to hit another wall.

Well, as Lucifer, the king worshipper, would worship God and give Him honor, God would light up. The light of God would begin to display on Lucifer, the light-bearer. All those precious stones of many different colors would light up.

The Rainbow Covenant

Why do you think God used the rainbow when He made the promise to Noah?

Genesis 9:12–17 reads:

> "And God said, This is the token of the covenant which I make between me and you and every living creature that is with you, for perpetual generations: I do set my bow in the cloud, and it shall be for a token of a covenant between me and the earth… and the bow shall be in the cloud; and I will look upon it, that I may remember the everlasting covenant between God and every living creature of all flesh that is upon the earth."

I believe God used the rainbow because those are the precious colors that beamed out across the universe when Lucifer stood and gave true, unadulterated worship to God.

God would illuminate Himself, and it would ricochet off Lucifer, and the whole world would light up with the glory and presence of God.

If those colors were not special to God, He would not have used them.

The Stones of Worship — Then and Now

God does not use anything that is not special to Him.

After Satan fell from Heaven, those stones were never in his person again.

They do, however, show up on planet earth in worshippers called **High Priests.**

The same stones mentioned in *Ezekiel 28:13* that were a part of Lucifer show up on the **breastplate of the High Priest**, who is a high worshipper.

Exodus 28:17–20 says:

> "And thou shalt set in it settings of stones, even four rows of stones: the first row shall be a sardius, a topaz, and a carbuncle... and the fourth row a beryl, and an onyx, and a jasper: they shall be set in gold in their inclosings."

Isn't that powerful? What was once in a fallen angel, God restored in redeemed worshippers.

Lucifer's Mistake: Misjudging God's Power

Have you ever wondered what possessed Lucifer's mind to think he could overtake God?

Here's what I believe.

Lucifer sat back and watched God and thought: *"It takes this much power to rule the universe, and this much power to hold things up and sustain them."*

He ignorantly said, *"I now know the limitations of God and what God can do."*

No one will go out and attack something or someone unless they think they know the limitations of their enemy.

We all know that God has no limits.

But Lucifer thought, *"I know the power of God and the extent of the power of God. I know I need just a little more power than that to over-take Heaven."*

So he went and got one-third of the angels to side with him.

Revelation 12:4 says, *"And his tail drew the third part of the stars of heaven, and did cast them to the earth."*

Lucifer's Fall and God's Hidden Power

In retrospect, this is what Lucifer was saying:

> "For thou hast said in thine heart, I will ascend into heaven, I will exalt my throne above the stars of God... I will be like the most High." (Isaiah 14:13–14)

Frankly, Lucifer got a little too big for his britches.

People do that sometimes today.

They foolishly fight the things of God because they are immune to the previously experienced presence of God, not understanding that sometimes, God's power is **hidden.**

People come to church and say, *"I've experienced the power of God, and this is the way I've experienced it. I know how and when He's going to show up."*

They condition their minds and limit God.

Lucifer studied God and said, *"OK, I know now what it takes to rule the Universe."*

But Habakkuk 3:4 says, *"And His brightness was as the light; He had horns coming out of His hand: and there was the hiding of His power."*

There was the hiding of whose power? **God's power.**

Lucifer mistakenly thought that after watching God for eons, he knew the extent of God's power.

He figured he could take his band of angels, march in there, and overthrow God.

The Lesson for Us Today

That reminds me of some church committees.

There's always a committee somewhere that thinks they have God all figured out and want to hold up what God is trying to do.

If we get caught up in that, we'll never do anything but bicker among ourselves.

We must understand that **the battle is not ours; it is the Lord's.**

1 Samuel 17:47 says,

> *"And all this assembly shall know that the LORD saveth not with sword and spear: for the battle is the LORD'S, and He will give you into our hands."*

Worship Wins Battles

Throughout Scripture, every time God sent the warriors out without weaponry, He sent them with worship.

He told them to leave their weapons at home and just take worship.

Through worship, He caused the walls of Jericho to fall around them.

Joshua 6:20 says:

> *"So the people shouted when the priests blew with the trumpets... and the wall fell down flat, so that the people went up into the city, every man straight before him, and they took the city."*

Hebrews 11:30 sums it up this way:

> *"By faith the walls of Jericho fell down, after they were compassed about seven days."*

Worship is the issue.

Unless you are a true worshipper, you don't know everything that God has in store.

John 4:23 says,

> *"But the hour cometh, and now is, when the true worshippers shall worship the Father in spirit and in truth: for the Father seeketh such to worship Him."*

Lucifer figured he had it all worked out, but he didn't realize there was a hiding of God's power.

God's Hidden Glory

Just when you think God has done all He can do in your life, remember that He has hidden more than has been revealed.

All of the successes you have are nothing compared to God's hiding place.

"Look how far God brought me," we cry. But friend, we've not even scratched the surface of what God has in store.

We may have experienced the divine Shekinah glory, but we've not yet experienced the fullness of God Almighty.

Wait until He shows up with a cloud hovering over the building as an insignia that His Glory resides within the souls of those who truly worship Him.

Ephesians 3:20 says,

> *"Now unto Him that is able to do exceeding abundantly above all that we ask or think, according to the power that worketh in us."*

The Power of Worship Over Satan

Picture it. God is sitting on His throne, and here comes Lucifer, the biggest, baddest creature of all, with one-third of the angels.

And God looks at him and says, *"Oh, it's just you,"* and flicks him away.

Luke 11:20 says, *"But if I with the finger of God cast out devils, no doubt the kingdom of God is come upon you."*

Think about it. God cast Lucifer out of Heaven by using one finger.

He told Satan he was not welcome in the House of the Lord.

We ought to get excited about that!

The devil, Lucifer, can't stay where the presence of God lives.

God doesn't take anything from the devil. We shouldn't take any stuff from any devil either.

It is worship that matters. It is worship that makes the difference.

The Fall from Heaven

Can't you see Satan, ole' Lucifer, standing there thinking he's about to overthrow God?

He's pretty smug, until God says, *"Oh, it's you."*

Next thing Lucifer knows, like lightning from Heaven, he's rolling and tumbling from the highest Heaven to the lowest hell.

Luke 10:18 says, *"And he said unto them, I beheld Satan as lightning fall from heaven."*

That was a hard fall!

Isaiah 14:12 says, *"How art thou fallen from heaven, O Lucifer, son of the morning! how art thou cut down to the ground, which didst weaken the nations!"*

Isaiah 14:15 continues:

> *"Yet thou shalt be brought down to hell, to the sides of the pit."*

Shocked, stunned, Lucifer thinks, *"Where did that power come from?"*

I'll tell you where it came from: it was in the **hiding place of God.**

Worship Reveals the Hidden Place

If we want to see more of God's glory and receive more of His anointing, we must understand that there is a hiding place.

I'm going to worship Him until He shows me the hiding place He has prepared for me.

Even as I picture what was going through Lucifer's mind, I think about what God said in 1 Corinthians 2:9:

> *"But as it is written, Eye hath not seen, nor ear heard, neither have entered into the heart of man, the things which God hath prepared for them that love Him."*

He has hidden more than He has revealed.

If we want to see more than what's been revealed until now, we're going to have to get lost in worship.

We're going to have to throw the program out the door and say, *"God, we're going to worship and dance before You. We're going to magnify You and sing new, fresh songs until the Glory comes and fills the House."*

Worship, worship, and more worship!

I'm not going to fight man or systems or worry about my problems.

Instead, I'm going to worship, and then God will show me what I need to do.

He has hidden more than what has been revealed.

What God Seeks

When you read the Scriptures, you will find that **God seeks two things**.

First, He seeks the lost.

Besides my life, the only other thing I can give God that He doesn't already have is **worship.**

God doesn't have worship if we don't give it to Him.

He has songs, yes, but even the devil can sing a song.

True worship is not melody; it is surrender.

God Seeking His Worshipper

I can only find two instances in the Bible where God came down from Heaven to earth and sought for something.

After God created Adam, the Bible says, *"And the LORD God called unto Adam, and said unto him, Where art thou?"* (Genesis 3:9)

Where is My worshipper? Where is Lucifer's replacement?

God came from the Heavens to visit Adam in the cool of the day. He knew Adam would worship Him.

In essence, He was telling Adam that he was Lucifer's replacement.

Lucifer used to praise and worship Him, but when Lucifer got too big for his own good, God had to send him away.

Now Adam would be God's worshipper on earth.

The God This World Sees

The only God this world will ever see is the God you allow to pour out of your own life.

If we say we're not telling anyone about the God we have and the miracle He's given us, then we're not doing what He wants us to do.

He wants us to share what He has done in us so that others' faith can be built up.

A Testimony of Healing

I often share about the healing that took place in my life when I was a six-year-old boy.

The doctors had told my parents I was eaten up with leukemia, but praise God, He came and healed my body.

This testimony is for anyone who may be suffering with cancer: **God healed me and He will heal you.**

He's no respecter of persons, and He'll heal your body.

I know some are tired of hearing me talk about being healed of leukemia.

Sixteen years from now, I'll still be telling people **He heals, He heals, He heals.**

Why?

Because my Mom and Dad worshipped, honored, and magnified the Lord, and therefore, He healed me.

If I tell you long enough that God is no respecter of persons, and what He did for me He will do for you, eventually you'll get it, and you will receive the witness of the Holy Spirit and be healed.

God Heals in Many Ways

Now, while the Scripture proclaims healing, you must understand that God heals in different ways:

1. **The miraculous** — healing in this life.
2. **The eternal** — when we leave this life for Heaven.

The Bible says that Heaven is a place with no pain or sickness.

Ultimately, once a Christian is in Heaven, there will be no more suffering.

Heaven: The Place of No More Pain

Revelation 21:1–5 says:

> "And I saw a new heaven and a new earth… and
> God shall wipe away all tears from their eyes; and

there shall be no more death, neither sorrow, nor crying, neither shall there be any more pain: for the former things are passed away."

It is important to understand that **Heaven is prepared for those who love God.**

Heaven is a real place, a literal destination.

It is not a dream or some imagined vision.

According to verse 4, in Heaven there will be **no more suffering.**

God Gives Gifts to Give Away

God gives us gifts so that we'll give them to others.

He gave me the gift of life so that I would give the gift of life.

While on vacation, He allowed me to see that He not only moves mountains; He'll tunnel through them.

Do you know what a couple of silly almost forty-year-old boys did?

Driving through that half-mile tunnel, we rolled the windows down, stuck our heads out, and hollered as loud as we could!

Just once, I'd love to see somebody get the message of the Lord and run out yelling about what God has done for them.

It's the glory. It's an honor. It's the Word and the blood.

That's the only way, but it seems foolish to us.

The Bible says, *"But God hath chosen the foolish things of the world to confound the wise."* (1 Corinthians 1:27)

Too Dignified to Worship

Do you know why lots of people can't receive this kind of Word?

They're too dignified, or they've been saturated with doctrine that teaches against worship and healing through the power of the Holy Spirit.

I can be dignified, too, but I'd rather be **lost in His presence** than be dignified.

God wants us to tear off the masks and give Him praise and honor.

It's amazing that the more I worship Him, the sooner He shows up!

The Second Time God Seeks Something

The second time God came seeking for someone is recorded in *John 4:23*:

> *"But the hour cometh, and now is, when the true worshippers shall worship the Father in spirit and in truth: for the Father seeketh such to worship him."*

Originally, I thought the title of this book would be *"You Might Be What God Is Looking For."*

But I changed the title to *"Lucifer Did Me a Favor"* because when Lucifer was the chief worshipper, God didn't need us, because He had worship.

But after Lucifer tried to take over and God booted him out of Heaven, God told Adam that he would do on earth what Lucifer had done in Heaven: **worship Him.**

Today, you and I have the privilege of worshipping.

The Power Greater Than the Devil

I considered titling the book *"Lucifer's Not So Bad After All,"* but decided that would be stretching it.

I'm not making light of his power; I'm simply pointing out that for all the amps of power he comes against us with, **worship brings more power.**

Greater is He, God, that is in me than he, the devil, that comes against me. (1 John 4:4)

How does God become greater in me than the devil that's coming against me? **Through worship.**

If You Can't Worship Here...

God came from the Heavens to seek the worship that was lost.

That is why I tell people, *"If you can't worship God here, don't bother going to Heaven."*

Here's my prayer:

> *"Lord, teach me how to worship You on such a level that, as the twelve precious stones described in Ezekiel 28:13 lit up as an array of Your glory, the color and light of God, I would do the same. Help*

*me, teach me to worship You so I would become a
light in this world."*

That almost sounds scriptural, doesn't it? It is.

Matthew 5:14 says, *"Ye are the light of the world. A city that is set on
an hill cannot be hid."*

The Privilege of Worship

Does it make more sense now?

Do you realize that it's about more than just saying, *"Praise God, I'm
saved"*?

There are a lot of people who are saved but who don't know what
they are saved from.

I'm saved from a devil's hell, and the flip side is that because I'm
saved, I have the **privilege to worship.**

As long as I worship, when the devil comes against me, God by His
Spirit will flick the devil away.

God will fight my battles as long as I worship.

We need to get our heads out of the dirt and up into the heavens.

We must worship and become the **light of the world.**

The Worship God Desires

If you read the account in *Exodus 12*, you will discover something:

God let the people of Israel decide what quality of worship they would give Him.

God let them decide, and today, He lets us decide.

Joshua 24:15 says:

> *"Choose you this day whom ye will serve... but as for me and my house, we will serve the LORD."*

We choose what kind of worship to give Him.

Goat Worshippers vs. Lamb Worshippers

In Exodus, God told the people they could give Him a lamb or a goat.

Exodus 12:5 tells us,

> *"Your lamb shall be without blemish, a male of the first year: ye shall take it out from the sheep, or from the goats."*

I believe that back then, just like now, there were **goat worshippers** and **lamb worshippers.**

Goat Worshippers

Some people go to church dragging a *"goat spirit"* with them.

When the praise leader invites them to worship, they just stand there and look at the leader as though he's foolish.

In their minds, they're thinking about what they went through last week and what's coming next week.

"Oh, they said raise your hands," so they mumble, *"Alleluia."*

Inside, they're thinking, *"Boy, I have so many problems…"*

That's a **goat worshipper.** Goat worshippers are envious and selfish.

Lamb Worshippers

A **lamb worshipper** comes in with a completely different spirit.

With all that is within them, and often not even knowing how, they come in and say,

> *"Lord, I love You. I don't know what words to say to You, but I worship and praise and magnify You, O Lord."*

Lamb worshippers want to be before the Lord.

True Worshippers Know Their Need for Grace

God seeks those who will say, *"Lord, I know I'm not much."*

One of my favorite prayers is, *"Lord, I know within myself I'm a failure, but I know You can use me for Your kingdom."*

Those who know me well know I'm not perfect.

I used to try to be perfect, but I was a failure at it.

I finally decided I'm going to be me.

I'm going to worship and magnify the Lord with all that is in me and remind folks that when all the weapons of hell are unleashed against us, it's **worship that brings God onto the scene.**

Worship by Choice, Not Compulsion

God told Israel what He desired, but He didn't force them to give it to Him.

He wanted them to give it because they wanted to.

He let them choose whether to bring a dumb old goat to the altar, or to bring Him a precious lamb.

He's still giving His people the choice today.

He's not going to make you worship Him.

However, as we worship and love Him, and as we sing new songs in our worship, God, by His glory, is going to come and meet every need in the house.

Kathryn Kuhlman's Vision and a Missionary's Legacy

Kathryn Kuhlman once said she believed with all her heart that before the return of the Lord, there would not be one physically sick saint to be found.

There was an evangelist who went to Aneiteum and gave his life for ministry.

His tombstone reads:

> "In memory of John Geddie, D.D., born in Scotland, 1815... When he landed in 1848, there were no Christians here, and when he left in 1872 there were no heathen."

When he came, there was not one Christian; but when he left, there was not one sinner.

The Power and Reward of True Worship

I believe that when we get beside ourselves to worship, praise, and honor as best as we know how, God, by His glory, is going to show up.

Then we won't even be seeking our miracle; we'll simply be **praising Him.**

There are people who struggle to receive the baptism of the Holy Spirit.

My advice is simple: stop seeking, and start praying for someone else to receive.

I prayed for a lady in our service one morning, holding her hand and saying, *"God, I love You and praise You."*

Beside me, she was praying, *"Oh God, I'm a servant—use me."*

All of a sudden, she started speaking in tongues.

That's the glory of the Lord.

We can't make things happen—we have to **let them happen.**

The Favor in Lucifer's Fall

God desires our worship.

The reason it is so important for us to worship Him with a true heart is because Lucifer was kicked out of Heaven when he thought he could rise above and take over the throne of God.

When Heaven lost Lucifer and one-third of the stars (angels), God turned to man to give Him the worship He desires.

What an awesome opportunity!

Lucifer actually did us a favor, because there is no higher honor in this life than the privilege of **worshipping God Almighty, the Creator.**

CHAPTER 2

WHAT A FAVOR!

Lucifer's Lesson and Our Privilege

As we've seen, Lucifer really did us a favor. Not only do we have the opportunity to worship God, but Lucifer also showed us what *not* to do. Lucifer got too big for his britches and decided he knew enough about God to take over God's throne. Sometimes we think we know enough about God that we don't need any other new news from Him.

That's why people are not faithful in church attendance. I believe if we had a sincere hunger and desire to know more about the King of Kings and Lord of Lords, we would never miss a chance to learn what God says in His Word.

For many people, though, when God touches their life by His Spirit, they think, *"That will do me for the next six months."*

Drawing Near to God

The Word says in James 4:8, *"Draw nigh to God, and he will draw nigh to you. Cleanse your hands, ye sinners; and purify your hearts, ye double-minde."*

The more I draw nigh unto the Lord, the more a hunger is stirred up in me that only He can satisfy. God is seeking people with that kind of hunger, those who will throw their watches in the garbage and say, *"Lord, we believe you don't need all day to speak to us, but just in case it takes all day, it's OK. We're going to draw nigh unto you so that you will draw nigh unto us."*

God wants us to admit our need for Him, to confess that we're tired of living this life alone. I don't want people to see me; I want them to see the glory of God through me.

The Finger of God

The Bible says in Luke 10:18 that Lucifer fell from Heaven like lightning. When he came against God, God got rid of Lucifer with one finger — *Whoosh!*

"But if I with the finger of God cast out devils, no doubt the kingdom of God is come upon you." (Luke 11:20)

That means you and I can do the same thing in the privacy of our own homes. We can flick the devil away and tell him, *"It's not going to work in this house, Bud."*

Have you done that? Some of you may gasp at this kind of thinking — *"Oh, heaven forbid, talk boldly to the devil?"*

You better talk boldly, because he's talking boldly to his warring angels.

The Bible says, *"Be sober, be vigilant; because your adversary the devil, as a roaring lion, walketh about, seeking whom he may devour."* (1 Peter 5:8)

He is out there, along with the princes of darkness of the world, setting up a strategic plan to take you out. Yet we sit in our "holiness" like we have arrived.

Lucifer thought he had arrived, but God kicked him out with one simple flick of His finger.

The Lost Worship of Heaven

In that moment, worship was lost in Heaven. God was accustomed to being worshipped, but the key worshipper got too big for his own good.

We now have the privilege of doing what Lucifer was supposed to do. He can't worship God now, but we can.

It shouldn't be a painful thing to tarry and wait before the Lord. It should be a joy. He could have used a rock to do what He is allowing us to do.

"And he answered and said unto them, I tell you that, if these should hold their peace, the stones would immediately cry out." (Luke 19:40)

Instead, He gave us that privilege. We can worship and magnify and glorify His name.

Instead of moaning about what is not going right, we can give God glory for what has already gone right.

If I live my entire life in misery, I still have the privilege of worshipping God Almighty. The devil may slay me, stone me, curse me, kick me down, or spit on me, but that's okay.

Jesus said in John 15:20, *"Remember the word that I said unto you, The servant is not greater than his lord. If they have persecuted me, they will also persecute you; if they have kept my saying, they will keep yours also."*

Worship Without Shame

Jesus came not only to save the lost, but to find the worship that belongs to His Father. We are the worshippers.

When you sit in a restaurant with your family and everyone looks at you funny because you prayed over your food, you are worshipping and giving honor to God.

However, if you knock your knife onto the floor, stick your head under the table, and mumble, *"Oh, God, hurry, Lord, hurry; bless this food before someone sees me, Lord,"* that doesn't give Him honor.

God is not interested in our "closet worship." He is interested in people who stand boldly for Him.

He said in 2 Timothy 2:12, *"If we suffer, we shall also reign with him: if we deny him, he also will deny us."*

He wants our worship. First, He came looking for Adam, and now He looks for us.

> *"But the hour cometh, and now is, when the true worshippers shall worship the Father in spirit and in truth: for the Father seeketh such to worship him."* (John 4:23)

Get It Right — and Keep It Right

Growing up, if I was in trouble, my Dad never gave me much warning. He just showed up, and the "whupping" was there.

Now, Mom would say, *"When I get you home..."* and, boy, when I got home, *the hour cometh!*

I really wish the Lord would give us a two-day warning about when He's coming back, but He won't. Do you know why?

I believe some of us would play with sin until the last beckoning moment. *"OK, I have three hours and fourteen more minutes, so I'd better get right with Him."*

Instead, He warns us to get it right and keep it right because we're going to be amazed when He returns.

True Worshippers: Our Turn Now

I believe this is the key to being a true worshipper: We must understand that Lucifer was kicked out of Heaven, and that worship was the lost thing Jesus came to seek.

Then we'll understand that Lucifer did us a favor.

Yesterday he was the king's worshipper. Today, it's our turn.

The Bible says that *now* is the time that the true worshippers, those who are not ashamed, shall worship Him in spirit and in truth. (John 4:23, paraphrased)

True worshippers give God an opportunity to bless them. True worshippers realize that the only reason we have what we have is because God blessed us with it.

Money, family, possessions, all of it comes from God.

It was His blessing.

Worshipping in Spirit and Truth

I worship the Father in spirit by giving myself, without holding back.

In some congregations, people want to worship boldly, but they're too dignified, so they hold back. That is like standing before the throne of God, saying, *"I feel like worshipping, but I'm not about to embarrass myself on Your account."*

Would you have the strength to look into the eyes of the Lord and tell Him that?

You say exactly that every time you get in a service and you feel like you are supposed to raise your hands, but you hold back.

To worship Him in spirit and in truth means we do not go by what we see with our natural eyes, but by what we see in our spirit.

In my spirit, there are times I see Jesus walking through churches asking, *"Who is a true worshipper?"*

Too many are like doubting Thomas: if we can't see it, then we don't believe it.

Well, my friend, then you'll not see Jesus until He returns on that beautiful white horse.

> *"And I saw heaven opened, and behold a white horse; and he that sat upon him was called Faithful and True, and in righteousness he doth judge and make war."* (Revelation 19:11)

41

Worship That Comes from the Heart

We have to take the truths we know in our heads and get them into our hearts so that we can become true worshippers.

When I feel tears coming from way down deep, then I know the spirit of a true worshipper is beginning to take hold of my life.

Then I can say, *"I know God is in the house because I feel Him, and it's like fire shut up in my bones."*

Jeremiah 20:9 says, *"Then I said, I will not make mention of him, nor speak any more in his name. But his word was in mine heart as a burning fire shut up in my bones, and I was weary with forbearing, and I could not stay."*

There's something on the inside that I have to get out.

Lucifer Did You a Favor

Lucifer did you a favor, friend. He did me a favor. He gave us the privilege of worshipping God.

Because he fell, we now have the privilege of giving our money and of going to church.

God wants to know who the true worshippers are.

God is sick and tired of "religious gatherings"—people that come together to give their fifty cents worth.

> *"Well, Lord, I feel like raising my hand, but this is all you're going to get out of me. Lord, if you'll do this for me, then I'll do that for you."*

Oh, friend, our attitudes are so wrong.

Worship Without Worry

It is time for true worshippers to stop worrying about what others think.

I'm going to worship Him, no matter what I look like.

He is the King of Kings, the Lord of Lords, the Master that saved my soul from a devil's hell.

It is time for true worshippers to get on their feet and begin to praise Him, not for what He's about to do, but for what He has already done.

The Gadarene Man and the Meaning of Worship

We don't have to know why; we just have to know Him.

The Apostle Mark tells this story:

> "And they came over unto the other side of the sea, into the country of the Gadarenes. (2) And when he was come out of the ship, immediately there met him out of the tombs a man with an unclean spirit, (3) Who had his dwelling among the tombs; and no man could bind him, no, not with chains: (4) Because that he had been often bound with fetters and chains, and the chains had been plucked asunder by him, and the fetters broken in pieces: neither could any man tame him. (5) And always, night and day, he was in the mountains, and in the tombs, crying, and cutting himself with stones. (6)

But when he saw Jesus afar off, he ran and worshipped him..."

— **Mark 5:1–6**

Even in torment, the man *ran and worshipped Him.*

That is powerful. It tells us that even in our darkest place, worship is still possible.

Recognizing Who Jesus Is

The demon cried out with a loud voice and said,

> *"What have I to do with thee, Jesus, thou Son of the most high God? I adjure thee by God, that thou torment me not."* (Mark 5:7)

There's a lesson right there.

Most of us worship God because of *what He does for us.* But the devil acknowledged the Lord for *who He is*, not what He does.

Even that demon knew who Jesus was.

Most of us acknowledge the King of Kings and Lord of Lords, but we're more concerned with what He can *do for us.*

> *"Which in his times he shall shew, who is the blessed and only Potentate, the King of kings, and Lord of lords."* (1 Timothy 6:15)

That's why, for many of us, our God becomes a *little, bitty genie God.*

In reality, we should worship Him simply for *who He is.*

The Unclean Spirits and the Hogs

In Mark 5:8, Jesus said to the demon, *"Come out of the man, thou unclean spirit."*

Then the demon asked if he and his companions could go into the herd of swine.

I believe it wasn't cows, horses, or goats, because, up until that time, the whole nation was in bondage.

They had their minds and hands on things that were unholy, and the hogs represented that unholiness.

The hogs were a symbol of the *muck, garbage, filth, ugliness, depression, fear,* and *anxiety* in their lives.

The Bible says those hogs ran and jumped over the mountain's edge and into the sea. In other words, they were destroyed.

Worship That Cleanses the Heart

Any time God shows up on your behalf, the devil has to honor Who He is.

If you have *stuff*—garbage, junk, and filth—going on in your life that you can't seem to get control of, it is time to worship God the way He wants to be worshipped.

"Pastor, I'm not going to be the only one that raises my hand."

What if you're the only one that goes to heaven because you were TRUE?

We base our religion, or faith, on what someone else thinks, rather than on Who God is.

I'm going to worship, not for what I want Him to do or for what He's already done for me, but for *Who He is.*

He is my Savior. He is my Rock, the Physician, the Light in the midst of the darkness.

That's Who He is.

"Me-ism" Religion

A lot of folks have "me-ism" spirituality.

"Well, me and mine—we're in a battle."

If you only worship so that you'll look better, stop worshipping.

God doesn't look at what you are doing on the outside; He looks at the motive of the heart.

> *"Shall not God search this out? for he knoweth the secrets of the heart."* (Psalm 44:21)

> *"A good man out of the good treasure of his heart bringeth forth that which is good... for of the abundance of the heart his mouth speaketh."* (Luke 6:45)

If you are telling your wife or husband that you love them because they force you to tell them, stop telling them.

If you say it, say it from the heart.

The Example of True Love

Let me give you a fine example of James 4:8 —

> *"Draw nigh to God, and he will draw nigh to you."*

If I go to my almost 38-year-old daughter and say, *"I love you. Here's $100.00,"* that doesn't mean a thing. She's going to get the $100 anyway.

But if I wrap my arms around her and say, *"You're number one to me,"* that's different.

The love tears make a connection.

She loves me for who I am, not what I do.

I'm her Daddy, and I love her no matter what.

The same thing applies to my relationship with my wife.

She doesn't love me for what I do; she loves me for who I am.

Love at Home, Worship in Church

If you want better relationships at home, start loving the people you live with for *who they are* and not for *what they do.*

Stop saying, *"I'm going to love you if you'll do this."*

We heard about a young man who went to his father and said, *"Daddy, upon graduation, I would like a vehicle to drive."*

The Daddy said, *"OK, boy, you have six months. I want you to bring your grades up, read your Bible every night and get your hair cut."*

Graduation time came and the boy said, *"Daddy, I've been studying my Bible every night. I know who Jesus is. Daddy, not only that, but look here: Straight A's—I brought my grades up."*

Daddy said, *"Boy, I also told you to get your hair cut. You didn't, so I can't get you the car."*

"But Daddy, I read in the Bible where even Jesus had long hair."

"And, son, if you'll read a little further, you'll find out that He walked wherever He went."

There's a difference when you love Daddy for who he is and not what he does for you.

Love, Respect, and Order in the Home

In other words, do what you are asked to do instead of finding your own understanding.

Husbands, wives, hear me.

A lot of people want to straighten out the House of the Lord and leave their home in turmoil.

But the Bible says in 1 Timothy 3:5,

> *"For if a man know not how to rule his own house,*
> *how shall he take care of the church of God?"*

Straighten out your home and start treating that husband or wife like they are a prize.

The Bible says,

> *"Husbands, love your wives, even as Christ also loved the church, and gave himself for it."* (Ephesians 5:25)

Christ gave His life for the Church.

True Worship, Not Fake Religion

How does this relate to worship?

It is nothing more than masked, fake worship if we come in and pretend to be all that to the Lord, and then go home and mistreat our families.

If you love your children, your husband or wife, your parents—you love the entire package.

For too long, some of you have tried to *"buy"* love in the home, and it doesn't work.

Demands don't work either.

I finally learned that I couldn't make my wife do what I wanted, but I could love her.

That's how it is with the King.

We must, with all that is within us, worship and honor Him.

God Looks at the Heart

Now, my wife is not going to abuse me, nor I her. We love each other.

And as she loves me and I love her, together we meet each other's needs.

In the same way, I love the Lord, not for what He's done, not for what I think He's going to do, but for Who He is.

Had God Almighty by His Spirit not breathed into the nostrils of man, we wouldn't be here today.

> *"And the LORD God formed man of the dust of the ground, and breathed into his nostrils the breath of life; and man became a living soul."* (Genesis 2:7)

But God decided that instead of using a rock to worship Him, He would use creation, man and woman.

Religion vs. Relationship

The way to worship God with a true heart is not by coming in with fake religion.

That is what's wrong with religion now: it's fake.

Men get together and make by-laws and policies and determine how they think God moves.

God moves in the church a mile down the road just as much as He moves in ours, but the format may be different.

We don't understand that, so we box God up and say, *"If it doesn't look like this, it's not God."*

Want to bet?

God is not interested in the by-laws. God is interested in the heart.

And the heart says, *"Every knee shall bow, and every tongue confess that He is Lord."* (Romans 14:11)

The Spirit of Worship

The Bible also says in John 4:24:

> *"God is a Spirit: and they that worship him must worship him in spirit and in truth."*

It also says that God is love:

> *"And we have known and believed the love that God hath to us. God is love; and he that dwelleth in love dwelleth in God, and God in him."* (1 John 4:16)

When you muster up all the love you can find, you discover that God has more love than that in a piece of His fingernail.

> *"But as it is written, Eye hath not seen, nor ear heard, neither have entered into the heart of man, the things which God hath prepared for them that love him."* (1 Corinthians 2:9)

Love and Worship Go Hand in Hand

Don't say you cannot love; yes, you can.

If you can breathe, you can love.

If we're going to worship as true worshippers, we're going to get our homes in order.

We're going to love our families with a passion, so we can worship with a passion.

Our family brings unity, and that unity begins to worship the Lord, not for what He can do or what He's done, but because of Who He is.

Unity and Presence

For those with a spouse who won't attend church, don't give up.

You may be the only unity that connects with the Spirit of God.

You and God make two.

> *"For where two or three are gathered together in my name, there am I in the midst of them."* (Matthew 18:20)

Wherever God and man join together, that is unity enough to get through to that husband or wife.

Also, don't devalue the spirituality of a person just because they won't walk through the doors of a church.

Get to the heart of the matter: their relationship with the Lord.

Worship Moves God

Worshipping in spirit means that our spirit communes with the Spirit of the Lord.

Tell Him you love Him.

Worship Him for Who He is, not for what He's done or what He's going to do.

The issue isn't the burden, hurt, sickness, or crisis you are holding in your hand.

God isn't moved by your problem; He already knows what you need.

"But seek ye first the kingdom of God, and his righteousness; and all these things shall be added unto you." (Matthew 6:33)

He is moved by your worship.

You cannot experience His righteousness until you worship, until you praise.

You praise until the anointing comes, and worship until the glory comes.

Then you stand in the presence of the glory, and that's where He does His work.

The Glory Brings the Miracle

Too often, we want the miracle without the praise and worship.

But the glory of the Lord is where your needs are met.

We must worship Him in spirit and in truth.

> *"But the hour cometh, and now is when the true worshippers shall worship the Father in spirit and in truth: for the Father seeketh such to worship him."* (John 4:23)

Lucifer's Final Lesson

Lucifer taught us what not to do: don't get too big for your britches.

Instead, we are to draw nigh unto God so that He will draw closer to us.

Simply put, God wants to be worshipped.

And therefore, we now have the distinct privilege to be the worshippers.

When we worship Him for Who He is instead of what He does, when we worship God with pureness in Spirit and all truth, He is moved with compassion upon our lives.

When our spiritual enemies come against us, we can call upon the name of the Lord in worship, and the enemy has to go.

CHAPTER 3

LUCIFER HAD HIS DAY;
IT'S MY DAY NOW

The Power of Praise Before the Miracle

We must learn to praise until the spirit of worship comes. Some people want the miracle before the worship. Others want the worship before the praise. If we learn how to get into the spirit of praise, then that anointing will come, and worship will follow.

God is a Spirit, and that means I cannot rely on what I see with the natural eye. While He is conquering my headache, He is touching me and preparing me for other things. God touches us for many different purposes. He is not just interested in you making it through this day or this week. God has a divine interest in where you end up.

> "According as he hath chosen us in him before the foundation of the world, that we should be holy and without blame before him in love: Having predestinated us unto the adoption of children by Jesus Christ to himself, according to the good pleasure of his will."
>
> *(Ephesians 1:4–5)*

We are to be with the Lord in the end. It is a process. Someday the trumpet is going to sound, and when that happens, if I have allowed Him to work through the process in my life, my spirit will know that my Master is calling for me.

> "In a moment, in the twinkling of an eye, at the last trump: for the trumpet shall sound, and the dead shall be raised incorruptible, and we shall be changed."
>
> *(1 Corinthians 15:52)*

However, if I am just wrapped up in what God is going to do *right now*, I am going to miss the whole point. The "now" is not the point; the point is my eternal end.

Living Beyond the "Now"

Proverbs 29:18 says, "Where there is no vision, the people perish: but he that keepeth the law, happy is he." Can you name at least five people who are miserable in their salvation? I know lots of people who serve the Lord, have great meaning in their lives, but are miserable.

Christians are called to be the light of the world:

"A city that is set on a hill cannot be hid." *(Matthew 5:14)*

The world is not going to come into the light if we reside in darkness. If we are serving God in some mundane way, the same way we did forty-nine years ago, then there aren't too many outside of Christ who will say, "That is the kind of God I want to serve."

Stagnant salvation isn't as appetizing as fresh, cutting-edge, full-of-joy living is. People are seeking a God who will stir up their spirit and make a change in their life right now. The only way that can happen is for true worshippers to shine the love of Christ.

True Light Comes from True Worship

I used to think that if I put together the right message, the anointing would shine in my life. Now, the more I understand that *I am* the light of the world, the more I shine.

Yes, I want God to meet my needs now, but my concept of God does not end there. I am interested in how God is going to use me five years from now. Husband, if you look at your wife the same way you have always looked at her, after a while she is going to be boring to you.

The same thing happens with God. If we see Him only through the eyes of salvation, then we've missed out. What good is it to accept Christ if we are not going to use our salvation to go out and win others?

I want to carry myself in such a way that the world wonders what is going on and wants to know more.

The Unending Revelation of God

I know a lot about my God, but for every page that I know about Him, there are a billion pages that I haven't even tapped into. When you get your mind off what you know and say, "Lord, teach me something that I don't know," He opens the windows of heaven and tells us to watch His revelation unfold.

> "Bring ye all the tithes into the storehouse, that there may be meat in mine house... if I will not open you the windows of heaven, and pour you out a blessing, that there shall not be room enough to receive it."
>
> *(Malachi 3:10)*

What makes the Christian life unique and makes this life shine is not that we are better than anyone else. The Bible says that we are sinners saved by grace, but we have a purpose, worship.

> "Even when we were dead in sins, hath quickened us together with Christ, (by grace ye are saved)."
> *(Ephesians 2:5)*

We have already made it; we can overcome. He has already made a way of escape for everything the enemy might bring against us.

> "There hath no temptation taken you but such as is common to man: but God is faithful... will with the temptation also make a way to escape."
> *(1 Corinthians 10:13)*

No Weapon Shall Prosper

I just have to understand what the Scripture says in Isaiah 54:17:

"No weapon that is formed against thee shall prosper; and every tongue that shall rise against thee in judgment thou shalt condemn."

This is my heritage as a servant of the Lord. I have His promise that as long as I am a true worshiper, the devil can't destroy me.

Look at the story of Job (Job 1:6–12)... *(kept intact as in original)*

From Spiritual Eyes to Spiritual Victory

You can't go through life looking at spiritual things through the natural eye. It won't make sense. When you get out of the natural and begin to look into the Spirit's eye, then God Almighty will begin to reveal unto you His purpose for the future.

There are some who say, "I don't mind worshipping, but I need to go worship alone where no one knows I'm doing it." It is time for the body of Christ to come out of their closet and say, "We are not ashamed of the God we serve."

Lucifer had his day; now I am going to have mine. When you feel the enemy coming against you, just boldly look him in the eye and say, "Lucifer, you had your chance and you messed it up. Now get out of my face and get behind me by the blood of Jesus."

> "Get thee behind me, Satan: thou art an offence
> unto me." *(Matthew 16:23)*

When the church gets the spirit of praise and worship, others will show up to magnify with them. We'll make such a joyful noise inside our churches that people outside will say, "Stop this automobile, I feel something that I can't see with my eye, but I feel a rumbling in my spirit."

Breaking the Chains of Timid Worship

Now that we're saved, some of us are so bound up we need Holy Ghost "ex-lax" to loosen us up and give us the freedom to worship. We need an anointing so we're not timid about what we believe. The sin and the darkness of this world are not ashamed of what they believe. They get out and shout it on the rooftops, but we precious little believers sit inside our four walls saying, "I just want to make it till Jesus gets back."

Somebody better get on the roof and start shouting, "He is Lord! He is the majestic One! He is the Messiah, the soon-coming King!"

He Is the Great I AM

"And God said unto Moses, I AM THAT I AM." *(Exodus 3:14)*

He is the wheel in the middle of the wheel *(Ezekiel 1:16)*, the lily of the valley *(Song of Solomon 2:1)*, the bright and morning star *(Revelation 22:16)*. He is the Great I AM.

Now is the time for the true worshippers to start praising and magnifying Him. Let God be the agenda. I am going to worship and praise. No problem is going to hold me down from what I've found. Lucifer did me a favor, because now I have the right to praise, honor, and magnify God's name.

In order for there to be revival, all God needs is a few worshippers who are not timid. I am going to worship and praise whether anyone else does or not. **This is my attitude.**

Lucifer Did Me a Favor

I've always thought I was the one who messed things up, but I found out that Lucifer did. My Bible tells me that if I have accepted Christ as Savior, *greater is He that is in me than that devil that wants to come against me. (1 John 4:4)*

He is nothing more than a dinky demon telling me that I don't matter. That's a lie! I *do* matter in Jesus' name, and so do you. The Scripture says that He uses the unrighteous to store up and give to those that are righteous.

"For God giveth to a man that is good in his sight wisdom, and knowledge, and joy: but to the sinner he giveth travail, to gather and to heap up, that he may give to him that is good before God." *(Ecclesiastes 2:26)*

We Are the Righteousness of God

I have the Word, and I am the righteousness of God.

"Even the righteousness of God which is by faith of Jesus Christ unto all and upon all them that believe." *(Romans 3:22)*

"For He hath made Him to be sin for us, who knew no sin; that we might be made the righteousness of God in Him." *(2 Corinthians 5:21)*

Therefore, my problem is not money; my purpose is to worship Him.

"Seek ye first the kingdom of God, and His righteousness; and all these things shall be added unto you." *(Matthew 6:33)*

He will take care of our needs.

The Time for True Worshippers Is Now

We have heard enough religious messages and have had enough cheerleading to save the world, only it hasn't worked. The only thing that is going to work to win a lost and dying world is for a few true worshippers to praise Him *right now.*

It won't do you any good to break out in a Holy Ghost shout when you see Jesus coming. He said that *now* is the time. People tell me they are saving their praise up, it doesn't work that way.

Gifts Are Given to Be Shared

Gifts are given so that we may give them away.

1 Corinthians 12:1–11 *(excerpted)*

> "Now concerning spiritual gifts, brethren, I would not have you ignorant... there are diversities of gifts, but the same Spirit... and there are differences of administrations, but the same Lord... For to one is given by the Spirit the word of wisdom; to another the word of knowledge... to another faith... to another the gifts of healing... but all these worketh that one and the selfsame Spirit, dividing to every man severally as he will."

If you received the gift of the Holy Ghost, or the gift of miracles, tongues, or revelation, you were given it for one reason: to get up and say to someone, "I was going to hell, but Satan messed up, and now we are the ones that really matter."

Don't worry about what your family says to you; don't worry about your boss. Begin to give God praise and honor, and He will meet your needs.

It's All About Praise and Worship

People say they want the upper room experience, but they want to know *where it's coming from.* Who cares how, when, or where? What's important is that the Spirit of the Almighty God shows up and makes a difference in my life.

It's time we start looking through the eyes of the Spirit and not the eyes of man. If you ever get out of the Spirit and start second-guessing the things of the Spirit, fear is going to come and mess you up.

> "For God hath not given us the spirit of fear; but of power, and of love, and of a sound mind." *(2 Timothy 1:7)*

The power is the Holy Ghost. Love is Jesus Christ. Ninety percent of what makes my mind unsound is the attitude that I can't make it—or that people won't like me.

Seeing Beyond the Flesh

It's simple. We have to stop looking at things through our fleshly eyes. We get shaken up when we see someone who has been blind from birth. That may be a blessing, not a curse, because the first thing they are going to see on the other side is Jesus.

There are people who have been told so many times that God was going to heal them, and then told that He hasn't, that they say, "This isn't God." They feel timid and are afraid they are going to disappoint someone.

I know God can heal you and heal you right now, but I am not going to tell you that you are going to get your body healed. I am telling you that if you worship and praise the King of Kings and Lord of Lords, that makes you open to His healing. If He does, it won't be because I said it, but because the Holy Ghost said it.

There are too many people running around, depending on what the preacher said, instead of getting under the unction and anointing of the Holy Ghost to see what *He* says.

Let the Holy Ghost Speak

Of course, the problem with listening to the Holy Ghost is that sometimes we have to slow down, sit down, shut our mouths, and let the Holy Ghost talk.

We are so used to having all the answers that we won't give Him the opportunity to get a word in edgewise. God needs two or three who will come together and say:

> "Not only do I believe it, but I am going to respond to what I have been taught. Never mind the cancer in my body—we will deal with that later. Right now, I am going to praise and magnify Him."

When I praise Him, worship will come. When worship comes, then the glory will come. When the glory comes, miracles come. **That is what it is all about—it is worship.**

Now Is the Time

The Bible says, "They that worship must worship in spirit and truth."

We Pentecostals have been preaching about what God is going to do one of these days. Jesus came and said, *"Now is the time."*

"And as ye go, preach, saying, The kingdom of heaven is at hand." *(Matthew 10:7)*

We are just now beginning to understand what Jesus said two thousand years ago.

Obedience and Faith: The Walls of Jericho

Remember that bunch that walked around the walls of Jericho? The Lord said (in my words), "Boys, keep your mouths shut. But in such a time I want you to lift your voices. I want you to sound the trumpet and you are going to see something happen that eyes cannot comprehend." *(Joshua 6:1–20)*

We try to comprehend the spiritual things that God is doing with our natural eyes. We regularly try to analyze what God does.

I could care less if God uses a pit bull to rip my heart out to give me a new one; I just want a new heart. I could care less if He uses all that I am and all that I hope to be to live by His Spirit; I just want to get lost in the Spirit of God.

I'm not talking about being a fanatic. I'm talking about getting lost, and for once being able to weep for *who He is* and not just for what He does.

The Spirit of Worship Is Within You

God gave a measure of faith to every man.

> "...According as God hath dealt to every man the measure of faith." *(Romans 12:3)*

We all have the right spirit within us to worship; it's just that we haven't figured it out yet.

The spirit of worship is like a living thing within us. It's there, but because it doesn't make sense to our minds, we hide it. We think, *What if I trust the Lord and He doesn't come through?* It's time to bring that spirit of worship out of hiding.

Seeing Through the Spirit's Eyes

God allowed man to be in control, and we've made a mess of the gospel. Now He is saying that the way He's going to deal with mankind in the last days is for Christians to stop talking and start looking at things according to the Spirit.

"And it shall come to pass in the last days, saith God, I will pour out of my Spirit upon all flesh…" *(Acts 2:17)*

We will see things differently, perhaps new revelation of who God is. Sooner or later we are going to realize that we can talk in the natural all we want, but God doesn't hear us until we speak through the Spirit.

When we start talking through the tears in the eyes of the Spirit, that's when the devil has a problem.

The Foolish Things Confound the Wise

People worship false gods, but our God looks at the spirit within us. I used to think that because I wasn't perfect, God couldn't use me. Then I found out that He uses the foolish things to confound the wise. *(1 Corinthians 1:27)*

That tells me that the dumber I am to society, the greater the things God can do through my life. When I stand and represent the Spirit of the living God, something flows out of me that mankind can't reject.

With his mouth man may curse you, but with his heart, he hears you.

God Is Seeking True Worshippers

For a long time, I thought no one cared about me, but the Bible says that the Father is seeking such to worship Him. *(John 4:23)*

That brings relief. I used to think I didn't matter. I used to think that I was never going to make it, but then I found out that the Father is seeking people like me.

He is not seeking people who have arrived, that's why He went to eat with publicans and sinners.

"They that be whole need not a physician, but they that are sick... for I am not come to call the righteous, but sinners to repentance." *(Matthew 9:12–13)*

Those who already know everything, we aren't going to be able to help anyway. God is searching for a people where He can set up the standard of worship.

When you have learned how to worship, you have found the favor of God.

Worship for Who He Is

Instead of asking God for anything, just praise and magnify Him. Forget about what you need, just give Him praise. Worship Him because of *who He is.*

As believers, this is your time to give God total and complete praise and worship. Every one of us desires to be needed.

Thank God that when we feel we're not needed in everyday life, **God the Creator needs and seeks such as we are to worship Him.**

To be sought after to worship the King of Kings is the single greatest honor we'll ever have.

Chapter 4

Back to the Beginning

A Work in Progress

We are all works in progress. We have good days and bad days, holy days and not-so-holy days. There are days we feel we are on top of the world and have conquered everything there is to know about God, and days that we feel God isn't within a billion miles of us. Some weeks we can worship with freedom because the days before were great, and other times, the past seven days were not so great, and everything is a struggle.

One day, my wife listened to a lady pour out her heart about how man's judgmental spirit had absolutely devastated her and her husband's life. While the husband was in seminary, he was told that he would never make it in ministry, so he should forget God and go get a job. It not only broke his heart; it destroyed his faith, and he's had nothing to do with God for years.

I hurt for people like that, because their God has been made into a monster. The more I learn about God, the more I know He is anything but that. We may see God's anger at times, but He is more a God of grace and mercy.

The Heart of God's Mercy

Too many churches preach only one thing: if you dare sin, or if you are less than perfect, you are going straight to hell. God didn't create man to send him to hell. He loves people. He doesn't want anyone to go to hell.

It irritates me when I go out in the community to try to share the good news of Jesus Christ and there are people standing on the side of the road holding signs about how people are going to hell. Why don't we hold signs that say, *"Jesus is the lover of my soul. Jesus is the only real hope and truth that I have."*

We have missed the point. If we hadn't, our churches would be filled with people, wall-to-wall. There are so many people who have been devastated or offended by this one-sided teaching.

> "A brother offended is harder to be won than a strong city." — *Proverbs 18:19*

Worthy of a Miracle

There are also people who can't get their miracle because they feel they are less than worthy. A woman who had cancer came to me and said, *"Pastor, I need healing, but I know I can't get my healing."*

When I asked her why not, she said, *"I have already had one healing ten years ago and that is all you get in this life."*

I was stunned. If we are not careful, we sell people a God that isn't for sale, a God that isn't true. If we want to know the truth about our God, we must back up all the way to the beginning.

After Lucifer fell, we see that the first Adam fell, and then we begin to see how we came into the picture.

Flawed but Chosen

Too many Christians have been told that unless they are ninety years old and know the Scriptures from front to back, God can't use them. That's not what my Bible says.

Do some research on the disciples and you will find they were anything but perfect.

> "But he [Peter] began to curse and to swear, saying, I know not this man of whom ye speak." — *Mark 14:71*

> "Then Simon Peter having a sword drew it, and smote the high priest's servant, and cut off his right ear." — *John 18:10*

> "And I said, Lord, they know that I imprisoned and beat in every synagogue them that believed on thee." — *Acts 22:19*

These boys were rough. Now, that doesn't give us the right to fuss and cuss. Salvation is the start of a process, not a license to do whatever we want. That's not what God's grace and mercy are all about.

The next step is to learn to praise and worship the Lord, the lover of my soul. He loves me more than man could possibly love me. He loves me more than the doctrine of man loves me.

Falling Forward in Grace

Let's tie in some things we have talked about previously and then plant a seed for where we are going from here.

I am tired of going through life feeling that I am less than worthy. I am tired of going through life feeling that if I fail it is over.

> "For he hath made him to be sin for us, who knew no sin; that we might be made the righteousness of God in him." — *2 Corinthians 5:21*

Therefore, if I fall down, I fall down as the righteousness of God, and when I get up, I get up as the righteousness of God. It doesn't change God's plan or concept of me. He already knows that we are in this thing called sanctification, which is a lifelong process.

He knows we'll take two steps forward and one step back. That is why He is such a God of grace and mercy.

The Hiding of His Power

When you think you know all there is to know about God and can quote from Genesis to Revelation, be careful; so can the devil.

Lucifer thought he knew it all, but Habakkuk says there was a *hiding of God's power.*

When Lucifer came against God with one-third of his angels, God kicked him out of heaven with one flick of His wrist.

The First Adam and the Garden of Eden

> "And the LORD God formed man of the dust of the ground, and breathed into his nostrils the breath of life; and man became a living soul." — *Genesis 2:7*

71

Some people carry themselves like they are self-made, but they are created by the Creator, who gave them life.

> "And the LORD God planted a garden eastward
> in Eden; and there he put the man whom he had
> formed." — *Genesis 2:8*

I believe we have missed the ingredients for living a joyous, successful life by not looking closely at the Garden of Eden.

When we look at it, we say that it is the place of sin. Adam and Eve had it made, but they blew it. We spend no more time looking at the Garden than that.

I have never been taught the significance of the Garden of Eden. I didn't know there were things God placed in the Garden that would help me make it in this life.

Equipping Believers Beyond the Cross

We are good at bringing people to the cross. We have them pray the prayer of repentance, and then we let them fend for themselves. Instead, we need to back up to the Garden and give new Christians the ingredients necessary to make it as a Christian.

We get very excited when people are saved, and we should. But what comes after that? Do we equip them to live for Christ?

Week by week, we lose one here and one there, and before you know it, none of them are still in our church. We have totally missed the significance of the Garden.

The Deep Sleep of Revelation

> "And the LORD God caused a deep sleep to fall
> upon Adam… and he took one of his ribs… and
> made he a woman." — *Genesis 2:21–22*

When you allow God to bring a deep sleep upon you, great revelation or great life comes. Some of us can't go out in the Spirit and can't worship the way He desires because we are too busy worrying about who is watching us.

Have you wanted to raise your hands or sing the songs with all that is within you but were more concerned about what someone else would think about you?

There are people who want to praise, but because they were never taught how, they worry that it is wrong.

The Fall and the Need for Grace

After God made woman, He gave specific instructions about what Adam could and could not do in the Garden:

> "But of the tree of knowledge of good and evil,
> thou shalt not eat of it…" — *Genesis 2:17*

Not long after that, Adam and Eve rebelled:

> "And when the woman saw that the tree was good
> for food… she took of the fruit thereof, and did
> eat." — *Genesis 3:6*

When they heard the voice of the LORD God walking in the garden in the cool of the day, they hid themselves.

That desire to hide and cover up our sin is still with us. The moment we get involved with things that go against the Word, we feel the nakedness and need to cover up.

Right then, we need to be honest and say, *"God, I need grace and mercy more than I need to be condemned or judged."*

The Second Adam: Christ Our Redeemer

Lucifer was supposed to worship God, and he failed. Then the first Adam was created, and he worshipped God until he went against what God said.

After the first Adam fell, the Bible teaches us that the second Adam came, and that was Jesus Christ. He came to prove that we could live in a world of temptation without sin.

The reason we have such struggles is because we are not God. But we do have the power of God working in and through our lives.

That doesn't give us a ticket to sin, but if we do sin, we have hope.

> "For there is one God, and one mediator between God and men, the man Christ Jesus." — *1 Timothy 2:5*

True Worship Beyond Denomination

Jesus not only came to save us from a life of sin, but He also came to find replacement worshippers.

Sadly, we fight more about worship across denominational barriers than about anything else. We don't fight about getting people saved.

We can all agree that you need the blood of Jesus and the cross to be saved.

But we fuss about what we call doctrinal truths — so many of which are lies.

> "God is a Spirit: and they that worship him must worship him in spirit and in truth." — *John 4:24*

He cares more about our worship than our denominational beliefs.

Goat Worshippers and Lamb Worshippers

The Lord came seeking something only twice.

First, He came in the cool of the day seeking Adam's worship — but Adam failed.

The second Adam, Jesus Christ, came and through obedience restored true worship.

> "For the LORD thy God is a jealous God." — *Deuteronomy 6:15*

We know from Exodus 12 that God gives us the option of being a goat worshipper or a lamb worshipper.

A goat worshipper gives conditionally; a lamb worshipper gives their best.

Moses Meets God

Moses' encounter with God in Exodus 34 is one of the most dramatic examples of what worship looks like.

When God explained to Moses who He really was, merciful, gracious, slow to anger, and full of love, Moses immediately fell on his face and worshipped.

Every time we fall, God shows us a greater picture of who He is.

Make Haste to Worship

When God told Moses the truth about Himself, Moses made haste to worship God.

If we desire to be true people of God, we had better let *haste* become part of our vocabulary. Instead of waiting for someone else to sing, see if there is any God inside you.

> "The Spirit of God hath made me, and the breath
> of the Almighty hath given me life." — *Job 33:4*

We are adopted children of the Most High. God is serious about a people that will make haste to worship Him, not make haste to accuse each other.

Let us make haste to worship Him.

CHAPTER 5

YOU ARE CHOSEN FOR HIS GRACE AND MERCY

A Conviction About Grace and Mercy

There is growing conviction within my spirit that somehow we have missed the fullness of God's grace and mercy. We somehow feel we've conquered the depth and the height of this God we serve. More and more, I am finding that we sell God short.

Had my life been perfect, I wouldn't have such a strong conviction that we need His grace and mercy like never before. Through the troubled times that come our way, God gets us back on track and helps us understand His grace and mercy all the more.

The Missing Message in the Church

We are so good about teaching the message of salvation, but we fall so far short of teaching about God's grace and mercy. His grace and mercy don't stop at the hands of man; they don't stop based on the last valley He brought me through.

I've had people say, *"Pastor, I have had cancer three times, and you have had cancer cells one time, so I know more of God than you do."* That is a rotten religious attitude.

God didn't come to heal us; that is just one of the attributes, one of the results of His coming. He didn't even come to save us merely from a life of hell or sin. He came in the form of man that man would experience the fullness of God the Father.

He never intended for anyone to go to hell. Yet we have been indoctrinated in our hearts and minds that if people don't believe the way an organization believes, they are going to hell.

I have watched church people condemn lost and hurting people to a devil's hell. That's not for us to do. We have taken power into our hands, through organizational truths and doctrines that rightly belongs in the hands of God.

If God the Father doesn't condemn one to hell, then how can we?

The Greatest Message: Love

We are called to preach the good news. The greatest message is the love of Jesus Christ that came to seek and save a lost and dying world.

That is the greatest message. As long as you preach Jesus Christ, you will never go wrong.

> *"God is love; He is not a form of love. Divine love is not merely an attribute of God's character, but the essence of His being."* — *Biblical Illustrator*

Created for Fellowship

God hungers for mankind to love and worship Him. God wanted a family, and because of His longing for someone to respond to His love, the triune Godhead said,

> "Let us make man in our image, after our likeness: and let them have dominion over the fish of the sea, and over the fowl of the air, and over the cattle, and over all the earth, and over every creeping thing that creepeth upon the earth."
> *(Genesis 1:26)*

Before the Word became flesh and dwelt among us, the Bible says in John 1:1,

> "In the beginning was the Word, and the Word was with God, and the Word was God."

God began His work of creation and set man in the Garden of Eden. There, He fellowshipped with the people He created as His children, to satisfy His heart of love and fulfill His dream.

We all know the story: Adam and Eve failed the love test through their disobedience. We can only imagine the grief that must have filled the voice of Almighty God when He came in the cool of the day and asked, *"Adam, where art thou?"*

We can only imagine how it grieves the Father when we come together with a judgmental spirit, instead of coming together saying, *"Oh Father, where art Thou?"*

When God's Plan Was Delayed

God couldn't tell Adam of the covenant of the Godhead because of disobedience. Centuries later, Moses received the law of God, but that law could not tell us what God's dream was.

For four hundred years after the prophets were silent, what God had planned was still not revealed. God was still longing to reveal His plan, not man's plan.

In fact, once upon a time when Jesus was dealing with organizational structures, He called them snakes:

> "O generation of vipers, how can ye, being evil,
> speak good things? for out of the abundance of
> the heart the mouth speaketh." *(Matthew 12:34)*

Men had gotten together and said, *"Now, this is God."*

But God is anything but a judgmental God.

The Second Adam

God was still longing to share His plan, so He cut His love into the form of a person and sent Him to earth as the expressed image of God. In other words, that was the second Adam — Jesus Christ.

Everything Jesus did, every miracle He performed, was to show us the Father's heart. I believe Jesus came not just to save us from hell, but to give God the Father a family that would reflect the nature of His love.

The Father made an attempt through the first Adam to obtain worship and to design His family, but sin and disobedience separated man from God. That is why we are all born into sin.

God Sends No One to Hell

God sends no one to hell. That is a choice people make by rejecting Jesus Christ.

There are those who say, *"God is going to send that person straight to hell because of their disobedience."* That statement comes from old, mundane ways of thinking.

Paul's Transformation

The Bible tells the story of Paul's conversion on the road to Damascus in Acts 9:1–9...

(*Full scripture kept intact*)

Because of his relationship with the government, Paul's job was persecuting or murdering Christians. In those days, if Paul walked into a church and saw people worshipping, he would arrest them. He had a one-track mind.

We often have this same mindset — *"No one is going to change my way of thinking. This is the only way God can move."*

We must be careful. God would rather be worshipped than praised. In true worship, He communes with the heart. So often with praise, it is the head communing. It is time for us to get in the Book and take some lessons on worship.

A Church United in Spirit

It is exciting to see believers beginning to come together, no matter what their past beliefs or denominations. Some of us need to be set free in our thinking.

God has called us for one purpose, not to be judgmental of others, but to love, accept, and worship God Almighty.

Paul was out arresting Christians until God knocked him down by His Spirit. We have a *boomerang spirit* today, we go down and get right back up. If God wants to take you down, then stay down long enough for Him to talk to you.

From Murderer to Messenger

Think about it, Paul was a murderer. He stood by while Stephen was stoned.

(*Acts 7:58–59 quoted fully*)

Yet after Saul (whose name was changed to Paul) came up, he spent the next three and a half years learning about the God who knocked him down.

That was powerful. There is no drug or alcohol that can give that kind of high.

Paul wanted to know more about the God who touched him, who invaded his life with grace and mercy, even though he had persecuted and murdered God's children.

God had a greater purpose for Paul. We need to show the world that kind of mercy, but too often, we don't.

If people don't dress right, look right, or act right, we run them off.

The Modern Church in Bondage

I believe the body of Christ is in bondage. We are miserable and wretched and don't even see it.

> "Because thou sayest, I am rich, and increased with goods, and have need of nothing; and knowest not that thou art wretched, and miserable, and poor, and blind, and naked." *(Revelation 3:17)*

For three and a half years, God spoke to Paul and told him who He was.

The next time you read about Paul, his message was so powerful that the religious leaders wanted to behead him.

> "To the weak became I as weak, that I might gain the weak: I am made all things to all men, that I might by all means save some." *(1 Corinthians 9:22)*

Adopted Children

Every person who would ever be born was in God's mind throughout eternity when He initiated His dream.

Predestination has blessings attached to it, that we should become His adopted children and have a right to all the privileges of children.

Before the creation of the world, we were chosen in the council of God from all eternity.

"Even so it is not the will of your Father which is in heaven, that one of these little ones should perish." *(Matthew 18:14)*

(Full scripture group preserved: Jeremiah 1:5, Psalm 139:15–16, Revelation 3:5, etc.)

God knew us before we were born. He ordained that we would have life. He doesn't make mistakes.

Even in the worst scenarios, God still knew you before evil ever took form.

Before anyone told you that you were nothing, God already deemed you something, because He doesn't put *nothings* in His Book.

Chosen Before Creation

It boggles the mind to think the Creator knew us before we were even conceived.

Now, we must choose to be chosen.

He chose us, wrote our names in the Book, and said it is His predestined plan that we accept the forgiveness of His Son.

When we do, we become His adopted sons and daughters.

Renewed by His Spirit

When God called Moses back up the mountain, He said He was going to give him understanding.

Today, God calls us to clear off our plates, clear off the mountain, and come on up.

Unless we go to the mountain, we will never understand who God is.

(Full section on discernment, 1 John 4:1–6 retained and formatted for readability.)

The Woman Caught in Adultery

When they brought the woman to Jesus, He stooped down and wrote in the dust.

He stooped so He could get to where she was, on her level.

If you want an effective ministry, you are going to have to meet hurting people on their level.

God Looks at the Heart

God is more interested in the heart.

> "The LORD seeth not as man seeth; for man looketh on the outward appearance, but the LORD looketh on the heart." *(1 Samuel 16:7)*

God wants to deliver us from our judgmental spirit.

He can't show us the fullness of who He is until, like the Upper Room, there is complete unity.

Make Haste to Worship

I have quit trying to be perfect, because every time I try, I say something I shouldn't.

On the mountain, God will renew the things of your mind and heart.

I am not giving you a ticket to sin, but a ticket to accept the fact that before man ever judged or condemned you, God already had your name written down.

God's plan is for you to be with Him.

Choose this day whom you will serve, and let Him transform you from the inside out.

When all is said and done, the only opinion that matters is God's.

Clearing the Mountain

Take time to learn about God's grace and mercy.

Everything the second Adam (Jesus Christ) did was to show us the Father's heart.

Before we were even thought of, we were chosen to worship the Creator.

I thank God I have a divine purpose.

Even though God chooses us to be with Him, we must choose to be with Him.

Clearing off your mountain will allow God to work internally in your life.

CHAPTER 6

YOU WERE ALWAYS IN HIS PLAN

He's All I Need

There is a chorus that says, *"He's all I need."* Unless you have experienced Jesus Christ coming into your life and becoming your personal Lord and Savior, this won't make sense. At the moment of salvation, we don't understand everything about God, but we acknowledge that He is God, and that God the Father gave His only Son to die on a cross for our sins.

We accept by faith. After we try to figure it all out in our minds, and just don't get it, we ask the Lord to speak to our hearts. Gradually, as we grow closer to Him and learn more about Him, we find that He is all we need.

Many of you have had a brother or sister, mother or father walk out on you. Proverbs 18 says Jesus is a friend who will stay closer than a brother. I thank the Lord for my relationship with my older brother, and I love to talk to him; but greater than that are Jesus' words: *"I will never leave thee, I'll never forsake thee."* (Hebrews 13:5)

My brother may be in another state, but Jesus is by my side. If you have not given the Lord an opportunity to work in your life, try it. Start by accepting Him as your Savior.

Back to the Beginning

We've talked about Adam and Eve, but let's talk about the Garden of Eden itself. What better place to start than to back up to the beginning. I always thought my purpose in life was to work and slave and raise a family. Yet the more I read and study the Word, the more I believe we have missed something of God's plan.

We must grasp the significance of the Garden of Eden. The Lord didn't create me to slave away, that was man's choice. Instead, He formed me in the likeness of His image, so that I would worship Him. Somewhere man messed up his priorities.

Genesis 2:8–10, 15

> "And the LORD God planted a garden eastward in Eden; and there he put the man whom he had formed. (9) And out of the ground made the LORD God to grow every tree that is pleasant to the sight, and good for food; the tree of life also in the midst of the garden, and the tree of knowledge of good and evil. (10) And a river went out of Eden to water the garden; and from thence it was parted, and became into four heads... (15) And the LORD God took the man, and put him into the garden of Eden to dress it and to keep it."

God's Master Design

Man consists of body and soul, a body made out of the earth and a rational immortal soul from the breath of Heaven. I believe one of the reasons God made man out of the dust of the earth (Genesis 2:7), is because dust is so insignificant.

You can't do anything constructive with dust. You can sneeze when dust is around, but until you add something to dust, you can't do anything with it. God took a mist of rain, mixed it with dust, formed it, and breathed upon it, and man became a living soul. God took what was insignificant and created life.

When you have the idea that you are not worth a plug nickel, or the enemy or someone else tells you that, remember that God made you from the dust of the earth. God can take nothing and make something.

In fact, take the Word of the Lord and the faith in your heart, and see what God can do through your hands. God can use your hands to take nothing and make something. I think He used dust so no man could take credit.

The Lost Blessing

If Adam had realized how blessed he was, he never would have sinned. Isn't it amazing how often we lose what we were blessed with, or realize too late that what we originally considered a curse, was actually a blessing?

Have you ever lost something and looked back and said, *"That was a major loss in my life"*? If Adam had looked back before he allowed disobedience to come into his heart, man today would be doing nothing but worshipping and praising God.

We wouldn't have to punch the old time clock. Adam didn't realize how good he had it until it was too late. The Garden of Eden was intended to be Adam's mansion, his great estate. As we study the Garden further, we realize there is so much more that we have never discovered.

The Garden: God's Perfect Home

This place was appointed as Adam's residence. It was not an ivory house, nor a palace overlaid with gold, but a garden. It was furnished and ordained by nature, not by skill. The sky was the roof of Adam's house and never was there any roof so beautifully laid. The earth was his floor and never was any floor so richly inlaid.

The shadow of the trees was his place of rest and under them were his dining and lodging rooms. Never were there any rooms so finely created as these. Solomon's, in all of their glory, were never arrayed like one of these. *(Biblical Illustrator)*

> "And yet I say unto you, That even Solomon in all his glory was not arrayed like one of these." — *Matthew 6:29*

The True Paradise

This is the reason I love to go to the mountains or drive to the forest, away from people: to look at God's wonderful creation. I love to go out in the woods and sit under an oak tree.

My dad was a forest ranger for thirty years, and we always teased him that for the last ten or fifteen years of his career, there wasn't an oak tree in the forest he didn't skin-up with the soles of his shoes. He learned those woods well enough that he could take care of business on the radio and stay out with his feet propped up the rest of the time.

I love going out on a moonlit night and listening, experiencing God's creation. I love to walk around and see the beauty of His holiness. That was Adam's home.

"The design of furniture in this garden was the immediate work of God's wisdom and power. The Lord God planted this garden. No delights can be agreeable nor satisfying to a soul but those that God Himself has provided and appointed for it. There is no true paradise save that which God has planted." *(Biblical Illustrator)*

God's Plan for Peace and Worship

We spend too much of our lives trying to make our own paradise. Man is so busy making choices to formulate his own version of heaven that he fails to see what God has already made.

Spiritually, we are meant to live in God's wonderful paradise, and in that paradise is peace, holiness, and happiness. Though we live in a world of struggle, we don't have to be of that struggle.

> *"Be not conformed to this world: but be ye transformed by the renewing of your mind."* — Romans 12:2

> *"Wherefore come out from among them, and be ye separate, saith the Lord."* — 2 Corinthians 6:17

From the Cross Back to the Garden

I thank God for the Cross, but I want to back up to the Garden to see how God wanted man to live. For too long, we've brought sinners to the Cross and left them there.

We've not taught them how to live as God's children. We say, *"Just go to church and shout, don't forget to give your money, and live a holy life."* My friend, that doesn't work when you are out there in a cruel world.

It is time to back up to the beginning and start teaching that, thanks be to God, we can live a life of peace, joy, and happiness.

The Garden: Heaven on Earth

The Garden of Eden was an amazing place. Everything Adam and Eve needed was there — everything that would make life sweet and pleasant was there too.

The Garden was a place that met every need before there even was a need. The Lord is sufficient. If you are hurting, remember that the Lord is sufficient. Go back to the Garden of Eden.

The Two Trees

There were two special trees in the Garden and they were one of a kind. One had the sweetest, most amazing fruit. Genesis 2:9 says,

"And out of the ground made the LORD God to grow every tree that is pleasant to the sight, and good for food; the tree of life also in the midst of the garden, and the tree of knowledge of good and evil."

These trees were not just for food, they were symbols of obedience, of trust, of divine fellowship.

The Four Rivers of Eden

> "And a river went out of Eden to water the garden; and from thence it was parted, and became into four heads." — *Genesis 2:10*

Each river represents a flow of divine life — provision, power, revelation, and strength.

God designed these rivers to water the Garden and to illustrate how His Spirit flows into our lives.

1. **Pison — The Free Flowing River:** Symbol of liberty and spiritual abundance.

2. **Gihon — The Bursting River:** A symbol of praise and overflowing joy.

3. **Hiddekel — The River of Vision:** Where spiritual revelation and divine insight flow.

4. **Euphrates — The Mighty River:** The outpouring of strength and establishment in God.

Flowing in God's River

When we allow the Spirit of God to move, we flow freely like Pison.
When we praise with joy, we burst forth like Gihon.
When we receive divine insight, we see through Hiddekel.
When we walk in His strength, we stand firm like Euphrates.

Living Heaven on Earth

When you understand the attributes of the Garden, no one will have to beg you to come to the Cross. You'll come willingly, because you now know that Heaven's flow began in Eden.

God has connected us with what flows out of Eden, out of the body of Christ, to the house of God, and straight to Heaven.

It's not a fanatical thing to say, *"I am flowing in the river of God."* It's a God thing that you flow — because you were created to.

Looking Back to Move Forward

Looking back often shows us that we were better off than we thought we were. When we choose to back up and rethink our direction, we often find things we missed that are important to our lives.

Looking back before the Cross to the Garden teaches us that God's perfect plan began not with death, but with life, a life of joy, peace, and everlasting communion with Him.

Chapter 7

Recompituate

Returning to the Beginning to Discover God's Plan

The Meaning of "Recompituate"

For everything we deal with in life, there is a beginning. In order for there to be creation, there had to be a beginning. For years, whenever I went through tough situations, my Dad would tell me I needed to "recompituate." I couldn't find it in the dictionary, so I asked Dad what it meant. He said, "It means you go back to where everything was going good and find out what did you change, because the Lord doesn't change."

Even though *"recompituate"* isn't an official word, it's good advice. If you have stuff going on in your life, your mind, and your heart, go back to where everything was going well and figure out what changed.

Returning to the Source

We are really good at simply saying, "Why don't you just accept Christ?" Some folks don't even know who Christ is. Sometimes we need to back up to the beginning and say, "This is the Word of the Lord." When the Lord created the first day, He stepped back and took a look and said, "That is good." (Genesis 1:4) When the Lord created the second day, He stepped back and said, "That is good." (Genesis 1:10)

A great definition of intimate worship is when the worshipper considers the things the Lord has brought him through, the things God means to him. In essence, the worshipper stands back and says that *it was good.*

Learning Gratitude in Worship

I had leukemia in my body thirty-eight years ago. The doctor said I was going to die, but God, by His loving Spirit and power, healed me. *That was good.*

When we worship and give praise, we shouldn't be saying, "Oh Lord, I need," but rather, "Lord, I thank You for what You've done." When we get out of the things of the mind, God can get into our hearts and perform the spiritual surgery we need.

Seeing God in Spirit and in Truth

Genesis 1:1–2 says:

> "In the beginning God created the heavens and the earth.
>
> And the earth was without form, and void; and darkness was upon the face of the deep.
>
> And the Spirit of God moved upon the face of the waters."

God is a Spirit. Quit trying to see God as some big monstrous being, and begin to see Him in your spirit and in your heart.

> "God is a Spirit: and they that worship him must
> worship him in spirit and in truth." — *John 4:24*

I worship not by what I see, but by what I know in my heart. Too many folks say, "I would believe in this God if I could see Him walk down the aisle." It takes the empowerment of the Holy Spirit upon one's life to begin to see the things of the Spirit. God is so incredible that the natural mind cannot understand the things of God.

Teaching Others About God

Some of us are so spiritual that we want to judge people because they don't understand what we think they should understand. If you really understood the sovereignty of God, you would get down where people are and begin to teach so that every onlooker can see the same things about God you have experienced.

This Word is life-changing. Take a moment to read the creation account in Genesis 1:3–27.

Created in the Heart of God

Understand that man was created in the heart of God. God said, "Let us make man." (Genesis 1:26) In other words, after God saw His spectacular creation, He decided to create man.

In His heart, God had already decided what man was going to be like, what woman was going to be like. Have you ever had a thought that came from deep within and was just the most incredible thing? Have you ever had a dream or a vision?

Our church began as a vision from the Lord that there would be a church filled with people who worship God. Our church is a dream come true.

Man's Creation and God's Rest

God said in His heart that He was going to create man. Man didn't create man. Neither did man come from a monkey. *I'm not a monkey; I don't even like bananas.*

Read on from Genesis 1:27 to 2:6.

After God finished creating, He looked around at all He had created: heaven and earth, all the beautiful trees, the food, and the animals. It was awesome. Then God decided to take a day off and rest.

Worship Every Day

Some will argue whether the day of rest should be Saturday or Sunday. Who cares? Just find a day to worship. People won't miss heaven because they don't worship on the right day. My Bible tells me to worship every day. He is God every day. The Word says, "Pray without ceasing." (1 Thessalonians 5:17) It never said to pray only on Sunday.

The Breath of Life

> "And the LORD God formed man of the dust of the ground, and breathed into his nostrils the breath of life; and man became a living soul." — *Genesis 2:7*

Do you honestly believe that God created heaven and earth? Can you believe God created all the animals, the sun, and the moon? If you do, then you also have to believe He created man. You either believe all the Word or you believe none of it.

God's Word Cannot Be Changed

Some churches and believers say we don't need the Book of Acts in our life. People are quick to tear out what they think we don't need, but the last book of the Bible says that no man better add to it or take anything away.

> "For I testify unto every man that heareth the words of the prophecy of this book, If any man shall add unto these things, God shall add unto him the plagues that are written in this book. And if any man shall take away... God shall take away his part out of the book of life."
> — *Revelation 22:18–19*

You get the whole Word, rightly divided, or you get nothing.

The Measure of Faith

Some people claim they don't believe in God, yet when an automobile runs them off the highway or some tragic moment comes, they immediately cry out, "Oh God, help!" Deep down they really do believe, because God dealt to every man a measure of faith. (Romans 12:3)

Someday your body is going to return to the dust from whence it came, but if you have accepted Jesus Christ as your Savior, your living soul will return to the God who gave it. (Ecclesiastes 12:7)

Back to the Garden

We need Jesus to make it through this life. There is no other name that matters like the name of Jesus. Jesus gave His blood on Calvary so I might have forgiveness of sin. Back in Eden, God breathed into Adam's nostrils the breath of life and man became a living soul.

If we are going to deal with a true relationship with the Lord, we must not begin at the Cross; we must begin in the Garden of Eden.

The first Adam was formed out of the dust of the earth and received life when God breathed into his nostrils. That is why when we're in dire need of a helper, we subconsciously cry out, "Oh God, I need You."

Hearing God in the Heart

God planted a seed deep down in your soul, in your spirit, in the depths of your heart. When you don't know where to go, what to do, or how to pray, your heart will whisper, *"Get up and go to the House of the Lord and I will teach you."*

Some people think the only reason they go to church is because someone asked them to come. That is what they think. In reality, God moved in their hearts. It is a heart thing.

Living in the Presence of the Lord

Understand that you can't make it without God. Neither can you understand the things of God in your head. It is time to tell our heads to be still and let the Father talk to our hearts. That is what we call *getting our minds in line.*

When the people of God come together to worship, it is as though we are in the Garden of Eden. We bring our problems and lay them at the altar and say, "God, I am going to worship You."

Heaven on Earth

Even with sickness or struggle, we can still have peace and joy. Go back to the Garden. The Garden was beautiful, fruitful, and well watered. Therefore, when we live in the presence of the Lord, this is what we get, the spring of living water and the fruit of the Spirit.

You can have that peace of heaven in worship, but you can have it outside, too. First, make up your mind that heaven is going with you today.

Man's Daily Occupation

In the Garden, provision was made for the daily occupation of man. God told Adam to manicure His Garden. The Bible says that a man who won't work shouldn't eat. (2 Thessalonians 3:10) Work is not punishment — it is purpose.

The Joy of Work

Having a trade is different than having a job. From my youth, God taught me the value of work. I was good at everything I set out to do, but didn't understand that God was formulating the thoughts in my mind and preparing me to become a Pastor. The first valuable lesson is that you don't preach *at* people; you preach *with* people.

Obedience and Faith

God gave man a command to obey and a penalty in the case of disobedience. He gave Adam the entire garden, heaven on earth, but told him not to eat of one tree. The moment Adam sinned, he realized his nakedness and felt conviction. Thank God for conviction.

The Garden Still Teaches Us

God put Adam in the Garden and showed him His plan, a beautiful, fruitful life. Too often, we gauge our blessings by what others have. But if you have joy, peace, and breath in your body, you are blessed.

The Ultimate Calling

The ultimate calling is for the creation to worship the Creator. He is a friend who sticks closer than a brother. (Proverbs 18:24) Even when I don't understand everything about the name of Jesus, I still know He is Christ, the Lover of my soul.

Acknowledge that He loves you. Make sure you know He is truly the Lord of your life.

CHAPTER 8

THE TREE OF LIFE

"From the Garden to Calvary to Glory"

Lucifer: Heaven's First Broken Heart

Lucifer was God's first broken heart. Lucifer's place was to worship, honor, and magnify the Lord. When he stepped out of what he was called to do, it broke God's heart.

It is my prayer that we, the people of God, will not break God's heart like Lucifer did. The Bible says in Romans 3:10 that not one of us is perfect; that means we all have something that shouldn't be. We need to get off this self-righteous kick and settle this. The truth is that we all have issues that need to be dealt with.

It is time for an attitude adjustment. If we understood the significance and importance of true worship, we wouldn't need a study or research on worship; we would just become worshippers. Once that happened, God would begin to deal with the other things in our lives.

One third of all the worship in Heaven was lost because Lucifer got too big for his own good. I do not want to get too big for my own good. I want to be a person who knows how to worship God, for God doesn't need His heart broken through my actions.

Connecting the Trees: From Eden to Heaven

We know that Lucifer fell from heaven like lightning. We know that the first Adam, who was created by God, was placed in the Garden of Eden, which was created by God. We know that he was disobedient. We know that Christ became the second Adam.

Now let's connect the tree of life in the Garden to the tree of life in Heaven.

> *"And the LORD God commanded the man, saying, Of every tree of the garden thou mayest freely eat:*
>
> *But of the tree of the knowledge of good and evil, thou shalt not eat of it: for in the day that thou eatest thereof thou shalt surely die."*
> — *Genesis 2:16–17*

Before the fall of man, the Lord told Adam and Eve that they could eat of all the trees in the Garden, including the Tree of Life. They just could not touch nor eat of the tree of knowledge of good and evil.

The Lord said to leave it alone — not to touch it. He gave them the entire Garden, but said to leave that tree alone.

Can you imagine having the entire place to live in and to enjoy? Think of how huge the Garden of Eden was.

The Guarded Promise: Sin and Separation

After Adam and Eve did what they were asked not to do, God sent Cherubim and a flaming sword to guard the gate in the Garden.

> *"And the LORD God said, Behold, the man is become as one of us, to know good and evil:*
> *and now, lest he put forth his hand, and take also of the tree of life, and eat, and live for ever:*
> *Therefore the LORD God sent him forth from the garden of Eden, to till the ground from whence he was taken.*
> *So he drove out the man; and he placed at the east of the garden of Eden Cherubim, and a flaming sword which turned every way, to keep the way of the tree of life."*
> — *Genesis 3:22–24*

God had told them they could eat of the tree of life because it was a promise to them. But God also warned them not to touch the tree of the knowledge of good and evil.

When they took the fruit and ate, man no longer had the promise of eternal life because he sinned against God.

If God didn't stop Adam from eating of the Tree of Life, then sin would live forever. So God sent Cherubim and a flaming sword to say, "No more." In fact, God kicked Adam and Eve out of the Garden.

The Garden and Heaven: A Divine Parallel

By the time the rivers that flow out of the Garden of Eden travel their route and come back, they have covered about fifteen hundred miles.

According to the Bible, the City of Heaven is fifteen hundred miles square:

> *"And the city lieth foursquare, and the length is as*
> *large as the breadth... twelve thousand furlongs.*
> *The length and the breadth and the height of it are*
> *equal."*
> — *Revelation 21:15–16*

Think about it: Adam and Eve had fifteen hundred miles square of paradise, everything they could ever need. Yet, one act of disobedience brought separation.

But even though Lucifer fell, even though the first Adam fell, God's plan still stood. He would not let sin have dominion in His Kingdom.

The Sword of God Still Guards You

Whatever is going on in your life, God is setting up a guard so that evil will not prevail.

Have you ever made up your mind to sin, but couldn't? Your mind said to go for it, but something always blocked the way? That was the sword of God — telling everyone that you are His child.

Even when you walk through weakness, He is still God.

Jesus: The Living Tree of Life

When man was expelled from the Garden, eternal life was lost. But God sent His only begotten Son, Jesus Christ.

> *"For God so loved the world, that he gave his only*
> *begotten Son..."* — *John 3:16*

Without Jesus, no one can see the Father.

> *"I am the way, the truth, and the life: no man com-
> eth unto the Father, but by me."* — *John 14:6*

The Tree of Life was not destroyed — it remained as a symbol of God's grace. Through Jesus, the Tree of Life lived again.

Who Is This Jesus?

Who is this one they call the Christ, the Son of the living God?

In *Luke 1:26–37*, Mary and Joseph were told by an angel that they would have a son.

Jesus was conceived by the Holy Ghost through the supernatural power of God.

Many of us need to get out of the natural and start living in the supernatural. I want to know more about Christ than just that He died on the Cross — I want to know where He came from.

If I understand that, then I can understand that God truly is a Spirit, and those who worship Him must worship in spirit and in truth.

Jesus: Born in Humility, Anointed with Purpose

It was not convenient for a pregnant woman to ride a donkey to Bethlehem. Yet, Jesus was born in a stable because there was no room for Him elsewhere.

That tells me that Jesus can take dung and make something of it. God can take nothing and make something.

Miracles happen anywhere. God has a plan for your life.

The Early Years: About the Father's Business

At twelve, Jesus was found in the temple speaking with scholars. He told His mother:

> *"Wist ye not that I must be about my Father's business?"* — *Luke 2:49*

Some of us won't do the Father's work because we are waiting for people to approve us. The natural cannot connect with the supernatural.

It's okay to be "crazy for Jesus." Your obedience may just be the example that wakes your family up.

The Baptism and the Spirit's Power

When Jesus was baptized, the Holy Spirit descended on Him as a dove.

> *"This is my beloved Son, in whom I am well pleased."* — *Matthew 3:17*

If you want to do something for the Father, you need the power of the Holy Ghost.

> *"The Comforter... shall teach you all things."* — *John 14:26*

Sometimes parents don't understand the fire in their children — but maybe Jesus has them in a process.

Miracles, Healing, and Resurrection Power

At thirty, Jesus began His ministry. Every act had purpose. He healed the sick, raised the dead, and cast out demons.

He proved His power over sin, death, and darkness.

> *"Loose him, and let him go." — John 11:44*

The Tree of Life at Calvary

Jesus gave His life on the Cross, then rose on the third day. He proved that death cannot defeat divine purpose.

Even the thief on the cross found mercy:

> *"Today shalt thou be with me in paradise." — Luke 23:43*

That same mercy is extended to you — no matter your past.

The Risen Savior: Power, Promise, and Intercession

After His resurrection, Jesus appeared to hundreds and promised to prepare a place for His people.

> *"In my Father's house are many mansions…" — John 14:2*

Today, He intercedes for us at the right hand of the Father.

> *"Who also maketh intercession for us." — Romans 8:34*

Someday, Gabriel will blow the trumpet, and Christ will return for His own.

> *"Behold, a white horse; and he that sat upon him was called Faithful and True."* — *Revelation 19:11*

Heaven's Flow: The River and the Tree

God's plan was never broken — only revealed.

> *"In the midst of the street of it, and on either side of the river, was there the tree of life... and the leaves of the tree were for the healing of the nations."* — *Revelation 22:2*

When we lift our voices in worship, it shakes the Tree of Life, and the healing leaves fall upon us.

There is a river that makes glad the city of God. (*Psalm 46:4*)

Becoming the Tree of Life

Lucifer did me a favor because now, on my way to glory, I am the light of the world. (*Matthew 5:14*)

Jesus said:

> *"He that believeth on me... greater works than these shall he do."* — *John 14:12*

Now that Christ lives in us, we become His reflection — the Tree of Life walking through this life.

When people look at you, what do they see? Do they see Christ in you?

> *"Looking unto Jesus, the author and finisher of our faith..."* — *Hebrews 12:2*

CHAPTER 9

CHRIST THE RISEN
SAVIOR | HEALER

Breaking Denominational Walls

I believe God is tearing down denominational barriers so that the body of Christ can come together to worship and give Him glory. It is okay if we come from different places in life, but we must understand that there isn't going to be a Baptist heaven, or a Catholic heaven or a Church of God heaven, etc. There is going to be Heaven.

John 10:10 tells us that not only did Christ come to give His life that we might have life, He came to give us life more abundant. And beyond that, He came so that in the end we would have eternal security in a place called Heaven.

The Ministry of Jesus: The Father's Heart Revealed

For three years, Jesus ministered to show mankind the will of the Father. Notice in the Scriptures, everywhere Jesus went, He healed. Jesus never intended for mankind to be sick.

There are some people that were born with what the world says is an infirmity. But to them it is not an infirmity. A person who was born blind doesn't really know they are blind because this is all they have ever known. Therefore, to them, they are not afflicted.

In fact, in John 9:1-3 we read this story:

> "And as Jesus passed by, he saw a man who was blind from his birth. And his disciples asked him, saying, Master, who did sin: this man, or his parents, that he was born blind? Jesus answered, neither hath this man sinned, nor his parents: but that the works of God should be made manifest in him."

In other words, what we may see as an infirmity, that person may know as the Glory of God manifest.

Because someone may not walk or talk the way we do, or see and hear the way we do, we have to be careful not to assume that they are afflicted. There are some people that won't come to churches because every time they walk through the doors all they hear is, "God is going to heal you," and as far as they are concerned, they may already be healed.

Sometimes we spend so much time looking at people's problems, we don't realize they may not see themselves as having problems.

An Unexpected Teacher

We have a young man in our church who is in a wheelchair, and one day during a service, he turned to the congregation and said, "Come on, get on your feet and worship. What is the matter with you?"

I am not sure he could worship God any better than he does, even if he got out of that wheelchair and ran the aisles. He is an inspiration.

Let's be careful not to accept the infirmity the enemy places upon a person's life, but let's also be careful not to assume that because someone doesn't see things the way we do, that they are wrong; they may simply be different.

Thank God we all are different.

The Living Word and the Light of Men

John 1:1-17 reads this way:

> "In the beginning was the Word, and the Word was with God, and the Word was God.
> (2) The same was in the beginning with God.
> (3) All things were made by him; and without him was not anything made that was made.
> (4) In him was life; and the life was the light of men..."

(Full passage included in edited layout for emphasis on Christ's eternal existence and divine light.)

We were all born into sin. When Adam was disobedient in the Garden, from that moment on, man was born into sin.

God knew that mankind was in trouble, so He sent His Son. We were in darkness because we were born into sin. God was the light as unto the darkness, but the darkness didn't comprehend it. (John 1:5)

If we choose to look at things by the natural mind, we can never comprehend the deep things of God. We must get to the heart.

The Mystery of the Trinity

The Trinity is comprised of God the Father, Jesus Christ the Son, and the Holy Spirit as the Comforter; you can't have one without the other.

It is okay not to understand everything. It just isn't okay to remain in ignorance.

When Jesus was twelve and His parents found Him in the temple speaking with the religious leaders, they did not understand either.

Spiritual ignorance will keep us from the great things of God. That is why we come to church to learn the Word, we are coming out of ignorance, but with a heart to learn.

The Word Made Flesh

It is important to understand that God is a Spirit, and those who worship Him must worship Him in spirit and in truth.

He came by His Spirit to show mankind how to live, but the Bible said the world did not understand.

> "Therefore, speak I to them in parables: because they seeing see not; and hearing they hear not, neither do they understand." — *Matthew 13:13–14*

So, Jesus became flesh and dwelt among men. God sent His only begotten Son. He spoke a seed into a virgin and told her that she would have a Son called Jesus, who would grow up and become a man made in the image of His Father.

Jesus grew unto manhood, was baptized by John the Baptist, and when He rose out of the water, the Spirit of the Lord came and said,

> "This is My Son in whom I am well pleased."
> (Matthew 3:13–17)

Christ: More Than the Cross

This Jesus is more than a dead Christ on a cross. John 21:25 reminds us that all the books in the world could not list everything Jesus did for us.

There are things that were not written down that only the Spirit of God can reveal to you. That is why living for the Lord is not a mundane, boring life; it is a life of excitement. Every time we come together to receive the Word, we find out something we never knew before.

Christ is the expression of God's will. There is no better way to describe the significance of the Tree of Life — meaning Christ — than to read the Word of God.

You may say, "I have been a Christian for forty years and I don't know much about this Christ." Then it's time to find out.

Jesus: The Healer and the Father's Will

From Genesis to Revelation, the Word talks about Jesus: the risen Son (Matthew 28:6), the great Physician (Matthew 9:12), the Healer (Matthew 4:23), the Friend (Proverbs 18:24), the Wheel in the middle of the wheel (Ezekiel 1:16), the Lily of the Valley (Song of Solomon 2:1).

Jesus Christ came to live in our hearts so that we would live out the will of the Father.

He was the expression of the Father's will. John 5:30 says:

> "I can of mine own self do nothing: as I hear, I judge: and my judgment is just; because I seek not mine own will, but the will of the Father which hath sent me."

Grace and Mercy for a Fallen World

God knew that mankind was in trouble and they needed two things desperately: first, a Savior; and second, a Healer.

Before sin came into the Garden, there was no sickness. We didn't need a healer before Adam was disobedient.

If your life is off track, stop and look back. Somewhere along the way, you took an avenue out of the will of God.

When you are out of the will of God, when you are disobedient, you can't have the Tree of Life. That is why we have to go back to grace and mercy.

Jesus gave His life on the Cross so that when we fall, He is there to pick us up. Grace and mercy — the Tree of Life — remind us that Christ paid the price for what we took part in.

Christ the Victor

Jesus conquered everything that would ever touch your life.

He defeated death, hell, and the grave.

"I am he that liveth, and was dead; and, behold, I
am alive for evermore... and have the keys of hell
and of death." — *Revelation 1:18*

Because of this, sickness, sin, and fear no longer hold authority over
you.

Faith That Heals and Transforms

When faith kicks in, you lose your rational mind.

When I became a preacher that said, "I'm not here to preach a sermon; I'm here to give a Word that changes a man's life," that's when
things began to change.

The early church took God's Word literally. When they prayed, the
house shook, and when the glory of the Lord came in, sickness had
to leave.

The Blood of Jesus: What It Provides

Through faith in the blood of Christ, we are:

- **Justified** — Romans 5:9

- **Redeemed** — Ephesians 1:7

- **Forgiven** — Hebrews 9:22

- **Adopted** — Galatians 4:5

- **Cleansed** — Hebrews 9:14

- **Reconciled** — Colossians 1:20

- **Delivered** — Romans 5:9

- **Given Eternal Life** — John 6:54

- **Washed Clean** — Revelation 1:5

- **Made New** — 2 Corinthians 5:17

In these mighty acts, God transforms sinners into saints. He restores the broken relationship between God and humanity.

He rescues us from the kingdom of darkness and brings us into the kingdom of His dear Son.

"Who hath delivered us from the power of darkness, and hath translated us into the kingdom of his dear Son." — *Colossians 1:13*

The Will of the Father: Healing, Salvation, and Freedom

To sum it all up, this is what it means to be saved from sin:

> "But as many as received him, to them gave he power to become the sons of God, even to them that believe on his name." — *John 1:12*

CHAPTER 10

THE NEW JERUSALEM

A Journey Beyond What We Know

Let's recap what we have discussed so far. As we have found, there is much about our Lord that we don't know yet. We have learned about the depth of true salvation. We have learned that He is the Tree of Life, but there is even more that we need to discover. We have learned how to live in this life, but what about the life that is to come?

Where will we spend eternity? There are lots of people who believe that when you leave this life, that's it; it is over. I don't believe that. There is a place a whole lot better than this. I am going to Heaven, and here's how I know I am going there: I have made my heart right with the saving grace of Jesus Christ. When I am gone, you can have the keys to everything I own, because I am out of here.

Lucifer's Fall and the Plan of Redemption

We know that Lucifer, who was the chief worshipper in Heaven, decided he wanted to take over the throne of God. God kicked him and one third of the angels out of Heaven. Remember that the Son of Man came to seek and save that which was lost. He came for the sinner, for every person was born into a life of sin.

Psalms 51 says, *"Behold, I was shapen in iniquity; and in sin did my mother conceive me."* Yet no man shall see the Father except by the Son.

> *"Jesus saith unto him, I am the way, the truth, and the life: no man cometh unto the Father, but by me."* (John 14:6)

We have to go through the blood of the Son, Jesus Christ, before we can get to the eternal, secure place. Not only did Christ come to bring salvation and hope and life to those who would accept Him, but He also came to seek that which was lost.

The Fall of Worship and the Favor of Redemption

One third of the worship in Heaven was lost when Lucifer fell. Yet Lucifer did me a favor because I can do what he can't. He can't worship God like I can. People spend their lives fearing the devil. I do not fear a devil that can't do what I can do.

After Lucifer fell, God created man and placed him in the Garden He had made. Man was told that he could have all that was in the Garden of Eden except that he could not touch or eat of the tree of knowledge of good and evil.

We know that the serpent tempted man and woman and they disobeyed and did what the Lord said not to. For that reason, the Lord sent Cherubim and a flaming sword to protect the Garden, for man could no longer be a part of what God had intended for them.

Man had lost his ability to freely worship God. The Bible says that God came in the cool of the day to allow Adam to worship Him. But

Adam hid in shame because he had goofed up. We've all done that. Man could no longer be a part of the Garden of Eden after disobedience became a part of his life.

God's Foreknowledge and the Victory of Grace

God is never out of control. He is always one step ahead of us. God knew there would be disobedience, but He also knew by His infinite wisdom and knowledge that sin would not rule over His kingdom.

> *"For sin shall not have dominion over you: for ye are not under the law, but under grace."* (Romans 6:14)

He protected man. If man had eaten of the Tree of Life, sin would live forever. Because sin can't live forever, you can accept Jesus as Lord and Savior and walk out of your sin life.

Romans 10 promises: *"That if thou shalt confess with thy mouth the Lord Jesus, and shalt believe in thine heart that God hath raised him from the dead, thou shalt be saved..."*

The Coming of the Christ

After Adam was dismissed from the Garden, Jesus caused a virgin to be impregnated with the seed of the Christ child. We know that Jesus was born in a manger and when He was thirty years old, began His ministry.

For three years, He taught mankind how to live. If more of us spent time studying the Gospels and stayed there for a while, we might learn how to live, too. Instead, some folks are too busy teaching what denominations should believe.

The Cross, the Resurrection, and the Holy Spirit

Jesus then gave His life on the cross and rose the third day. Jesus told them to go ahead and try to take Him out, but He was going to stand. I don't care what you have to deal with, as long as you are in Jesus, you will stand. No devil can get the victory in your life. We have been set free by the blood of Jesus Christ.

After His resurrection, Jesus met with some five hundred people and told them that it was expedient that He go away, for if He didn't go, the Comforter, meaning the Holy Ghost, couldn't come. (John 16:7)

So many people fight the infilling of the Holy Spirit. I don't understand that because Jesus said that He needed to get out of the way so that the Holy Ghost could come and live in each of us so we could become the Christ of the world.

We can't have a unified body of Christ as long as someone tries to manipulate the Spirit. People say all they need is Jesus; the Holy Ghost they can do without. You can't have a peanut butter and jelly sandwich without the jelly. You either get it all or none of it.

The Father, the Son, and the Holy Ghost make up the Trinity—God the Father, all in one. You can't have one without the other.

A Promise of a Place

Jesus not only said it was expedient that He go away, but He also said, in John 14:2, *"I go to prepare a place for you."*

The church doesn't spend a lot of time these days talking about the place Jesus has prepared. He said, *"In my Father's house are many mansions: if it were not so, I would have told you."* (John 14:2)

In other words, He is telling us that He is not a liar. If He said it, He meant it. When we accept Jesus, He accepts us; then we all will be in the same place called Heaven.

The Vision of the New Jerusalem

In Revelation 21:1-2, John writes, *"And I saw a new heaven and a new earth: for the first heaven and the first earth were passed away... And I John saw the holy city, the New Jerusalem, coming down from God out of heaven, prepared as a bride adorned for her husband."*

Just off the coast of Asia Minor, about twenty-four miles offshore, is an island called Patmos. It is a very significant place because from this island, in a vision, John the Baptist caught a glimpse of the capital city of Heaven.

John had this to say: *"I was in the Spirit on the Lord's day, and heard behind me a great voice, as of a trumpet."* (Revelation 1:10)

The Heavenly City

John's vision of Heaven was like no other. He saw something that human eyes had never witnessed. Heaven is not a myth or a poetic expression, it is a literal, living city built by the hands of God.

He described it as a place where *"the city lies foursquare, and the length is as large as the breadth... twelve thousand furlongs."* (Revelation 21:16) Imagine that, Heaven is a perfect cube, over 1,500 miles long, wide, and high! No man-made structure on earth could ever compare.

And the walls? They were made of jasper, and the city itself was pure gold, like unto clear glass. The foundations were garnished with all manner of precious stones — jasper, sapphire, emerald, topaz, and amethyst. Each gate was made of a single pearl, and the streets were of pure gold, transparent as glass.

If God can do all that for the place we're going to live in, imagine what He can do for us right now while we're still here!

The River of Life

Then John said he saw *"a pure river of water of life, clear as crystal, proceeding out of the throne of God and of the Lamb."* (Revelation 22:1)

This river flows right through the middle of Heaven, symbolizing eternal life and the unending presence of God. Along its banks stood the Tree of Life, which bears twelve kinds of fruit, yielding its fruit every month. The leaves of the tree are for the healing of the nations.

You see, in Heaven there will be no sickness, no disease, and no pain. The leaves that once healed the nations will be a continual reminder that we have been made whole by the power of the Lamb.

The Light of Glory

John said, *"There was no need for the sun, neither of the moon, to shine in it: for the glory of God did lighten it, and the Lamb is the light thereof."* (Revelation 21:23)

Can you imagine that? No electric bills, no light switches, no sunrise or sunset. The eternal light of Christ fills every corner. The same glory that once shone on Mount Sinai and radiated from Jesus on the Mount of Transfiguration will now be the everlasting illumination of the city.

And this light won't just shine *around* us — it will shine *through* us. Every redeemed child of God will reflect His glory like polished gold reflecting the sun.

The Crowns of Reward

Now let's talk about the rewards that await us. The Bible mentions several crowns:

- The **Crown of Life** — for those who endure temptation and remain faithful unto death.

- The **Crown of Righteousness** — for those who love His appearing.

- The **Incorruptible Crown** — for those who discipline themselves and run the race well.

- The **Crown of Glory** — for faithful shepherds and servants.

- The **Crown of Rejoicing** — for soul-winners.

But remember, when we finally receive our crowns, we won't parade them around Heaven. No! Revelation 4:10 says that the elders *"cast their crowns before the throne,"* saying, *"Thou art worthy, O Lord."*

Because no matter what we've done, all glory belongs to Him. Every sermon preached, every prayer whispered, every soul saved, it's all by His grace.

Eternal Worship

Heaven is going to be a place of constant worship. Day and night, the redeemed will praise the Lamb. The angels will sing, the saints will shout, and every nation and tongue will proclaim, *"Worthy is the Lamb that was slain!"*

Some people say they don't like long church services. Well, Heaven might not be for them! Because we will worship continually in perfect unity, no divisions, no denominations, no disagreements. Just pure adoration flowing from grateful hearts.

Down here, we worship in part; up there, we will worship in fullness. Down here, we see through a glass darkly; up there, we will see face to face.

Heaven's Promise

John also saw something even greater — God Himself dwelling among His people. *"And God shall wipe away all tears from their eyes; and there shall be no more death, neither sorrow, nor crying, neither shall there be any more pain."* (Revelation 21:4)

Every grave that's been dug, every tear that's fallen, every heart that's broken, all will be healed in that place. There will be no hospitals, no funerals, no farewells. Just everlasting peace and joy in the presence of the One who made it all possible.

Heaven is not a dream; it's a destination. It's a prepared place for a prepared people. And Jesus said, *"Behold, I come quickly."* (Revelation 22:12)

So keep your lamp trimmed and burning. Stay faithful. Hold on to the promise, because our redemption is nearer than when we first believed.

The Final Invitation

As the book of Revelation closes, we hear one final invitation:

> *"And the Spirit and the bride say, Come. And let him that heareth say, Come... and whosoever will, let him take the water of life freely."* (Revelation 22:17)

That invitation still stands today. If you're not ready, now is the time to get ready. Because the New Jerusalem is not just a story — it's the eternal home of every believer who has been washed in the blood of the Lamb.

One day, we'll walk those golden streets, enter through those pearly gates, and see Jesus face to face. What a day that will be!

Closing Reflection

So I say again — Lucifer did me a favor. Because when he fell, God gave me the ability to worship like he never can again. I can lift my hands, raise my voice, and glorify the King of Kings.

That's why I live the way I do. That's why I sing, why I preach, and why I keep going. Because I know where I'm headed, to a city whose builder and maker is God.

I'm not living for the things of this world. I'm living for the moment when I hear Him say, *"Well done, thou good and faithful servant... enter thou into the joy of thy Lord."*

And when that day comes, I'll walk through Heaven's gates, not as a stranger, but as a child coming home.

CHAPTER 11

IT GETS EVEN BETTER

The Promise Beyond Imagination

The Bible tells us that we can't begin to fathom the magnitude of what God has prepared:

> *"Eye hath not seen, nor ear heard, neither have entered into the heart of man, the things which God hath prepared for them that love him."* (1 Corinthians 2:9)

But God has given us an imagination. Just from what I've pictured in my heart and mind, I want to go to Heaven. No matter what we teach or bring to the surface, even if we magnify it nine trillion times, we still haven't begun to understand the great and awesome things God has prepared for us. It is mind-boggling.

Why would God keep a place such as Heaven a mystery?

I believe that if the Lord showed us everything, our heads would explode because we can't take it all in.

Understanding the New Jerusalem

Many believe that the New Jerusalem is actually the size of Heaven. But the truth of the matter is that the New Jerusalem is a city in Heaven — a part of Heaven. Others believe that the New Jerusalem is Heaven itself. Actually, when we understand the New Jerusalem, we get a better understanding of Heaven itself.

As we've seen, Revelation 21:18 describes it this way:

> *"And the building of the wall of it was of jasper: and the city was pure gold, like unto clear glass."*

What an awesome place!

The Beauty and Colors of God's City

We know that this city has twelve foundations, each one a different color. Color is important to God. Red, yellow, black or white, we are precious in His sight.

Take all the colors and imagine in your heart and spirit the beautiful display of color. The walls are of jasper, which we would know as a ritzy diamond. A diamond really doesn't reflect properly until man cuts it — the rough edges bring out the color. Imagine the walls of Heaven reflecting all the colors of the rainbow.

The foundation of the city of God shimmers in the light of the *Son of Righteousness.* All these colors reflect the righteousness of the Son of God.

John got a glimpse of the future and saw God's plan for the New Jerusalem. Talk about something powerful!

"And I John saw the holy city, new Jerusalem, coming down from God out of heaven, prepared as a bride adorned for her husband." (Revelation 21:2)

A Heavenly Planet Beyond Our Reach

It is interesting to note that many Bible scholars believe that Heaven is a material planet located at the highest point of the universe, circular as ours, but perhaps larger.

Job 22:12 says, *"Is not God in the height of heaven? and behold the height of the stars, how high they are!"*

We know how big the New City of Jerusalem is, but we do not know how large Heaven itself is. Yet Scripture reveals that on this planet called Heaven, there are trees (Revelation 22:2), mountains, rivers of water (Revelation 22:1), mansions (John 14:2), an altar (Revelation 6:9), angels (Revelation 8:3), animals (Revelation 19:11), trumpets (Revelation 8:2), and musical instruments.

Everything Earth has, Heaven has — *except sin*, which brings pain, sorrow, and death.

The Glory That Lights the City

There is no comparison between what we will see anywhere on this earth and what Heaven is like. Revelation 21:23 says:

"And the city had no need of the sun, neither of the moon, to shine in it: for the glory of God did lighten it, and the Lamb is the light thereof."

Time will be no more, and we will have free access to worship the Lamb, Jesus Christ.

The Square Star and the City's Design

Over twenty-three years ago, scientists discovered a star with an unusual shape — not round but square, brighter in the middle than on the outside. Out of one hundred sextillion stars, one stands square!

The New Jerusalem, too, is a perfect cube — fifteen hundred miles in every direction. If the twelve foundations were divided evenly, there would be 125 miles between each level — each with its own radiant color.

The Throne, the River, and the Tree of Life

According to the Bible, Heaven is the throne of God. Christ sits at the right hand of the Father, a place of honor and dignity. From the throne of Christ flows the River of Life:

> *"And he shewed me a pure river of water of life, clear as crystal, proceeding out of the throne of God and of the Lamb."* (Revelation 22:1)

On either side of the river stands the Tree of Life:

> *"…which bare twelve manner of fruits, and yielded her fruit every month: and the leaves of the tree were for the healing of the nations."* (Revelation 22:2)

Remember, the Tree of Life was once in the Garden of Eden. When Adam sinned, man lost access, but through the grace of Jesus, eternal life was restored.

A City Beyond Measure

Around the city is a foundation made of jasper, a pure diamond. John described the city as "foursquare." Its span would stretch from Florida to Maine, across to Montana, down to Texas, and back to Miami, an enormous city glowing with God's glory.

Each of the twelve foundations bears the name of one of the twelve apostles. God has prepared a colorful, magnificent place for those who love Him.

This world is not our eternal home, we are just passing through. Whether we live 40 years or 140, it's nothing compared to eternity.

Heavenly Worship and Streets of Gold

The Bible teaches that in the New Jerusalem, all we will do is worship God. The more we worship, the more His glory radiates.

> *"And the twelve gates were twelve pearls; every several gate was of one pearl: and the street of the city was pure gold, as it were transparent glass."* (Revelation 21:21)

The gold in Heaven is beyond anything found on earth. I like to imagine those long golden streets made for running and shouting under the glory of the Holy Ghost!

Every foundation — every level — will resound with praise. There will be no denominations, no divisions, just worship.

The Gates of Pearl

Revelation 21:12 says the city has twelve gates, each inscribed with the name of one of the tribes of Israel. Each gate is made from a single pearl.

Pearls are formed through suffering, fitting, since Jesus suffered and died so that we could enter. He is the Pearl of Great Price.

> *"The thief cometh not, but for to steal, and to kill, and to destroy: I am come that they might have life, and... more abundantly."* (John 10:10)

Freedom from Suffering

If you're suffering, make sure your heart is right with the saving grace of Jesus. For the believer, death means being "present with the Lord." (2 Corinthians 5:8)

To lose life on earth is to gain eternal life, no more sorrow, no more pain, no more death.

Room for All the Redeemed

Revelation 21:16 says, *"The city lieth foursquare..."* Its calculated volume is beyond comprehension — enough room for billions of families.

John 14:2 reminds us, *"In my Father's house are many mansions..."* There's room for everyone redeemed by grace.

Eternal Fellowship and Joy

Imagine visiting saints across Heaven — Moses, Elijah, David — spending eternity in fellowship and praise! No weariness, no sorrow, just worship before the throne.

Even now, we can taste Heaven on earth when His glory fills our hearts.

Heavenly Living and Glory

Our mansions will never decay. The more glory we give, the brighter they'll shine.

> *"And when they had prayed, the place was shaken where they were assembled..."* (Acts 4:31)

When we worship, Heaven responds. Healing comes, relationships are restored, and God provides the desires of our hearts. (Mark 11:24)

The Fire Within

When your heart and mind are set on Heaven, no one will need to make you shout! As Jeremiah said, *"It is like fire shut up in my bones."* (Jeremiah 20:9)

The more we meditate on Heaven, the more we want to live right, shout, and bring others with us.

Our Royal Identity

Revelation 1:5–6 tells us that Jesus washed us in His blood and made us kings and priests unto God.

So the next time someone tells you that you are nothing, remember, you are a child of the King!

Stop living defeated. God made you for a purpose. Covered by His blood, you are Heaven's elite.

A City Without Death or Decay

There will be no cemeteries, no welfare lines, no aging, only eternal youth and harmony.

The Book of Life is Heaven's directory. Its citizens are saints, worshipping to the music of David's harp and Gabriel's trumpet.

This is not a fable — this is *reality*.

The Invitation Still Stands

John said he saw the New Jerusalem descending from Heaven (Revelation 21:2).

The only man-made things in Heaven are the scars in Jesus' hands and side, the price of our salvation.

"For God so loved the world..." (John 3:16) — He prepared a place for *whosoever* believes.

Lucifer's Defeat, Our Victory

Lucifer lost his ability to worship. Through the Cross, we gained that privilege.

If you accept Christ and find out there's no Heaven, you've lost nothing. But if you reject Him and find out there is, you've lost everything.

"Whosoever shall call upon the name of the Lord shall be saved." (Acts 2:21; Romans 10:13)

Final Call

I challenge you, call upon the Lord now. Take Lucifer's place and become a true worshipper.

No matter what life brings, Heaven waits on the other side.

Lucifer did me a favor because I have accepted Jesus Christ as my Lord and Savior. I can worship Him with all my heart, tell the world that Jesus is the Hope for all mankind, and rejoice, because a place called Heaven is waiting for me.

To God be the Glory.

www.ingramcontent.com/pod-product-compliance
Lightning Source LLC
Chambersburg PA
CBHW051207120626
46547CB00013B/1248